Implementing Decision Support Syst
Techniques and Tools

INFORMATION SYSTEMS SERIES

Consulting Editors

D.E. AVISON
BA, MSc, PHD, FBCS

Professor of Information Systems
Department of Accounting
and Management Science
Southampton University, UK

G. FITZGERALD
BA, MSc, MBCS

Professor of Information Systems
Department of Information Systems and Computing
Brunel University, UK

This series of student and postgraduate texts covers a wide variety of topics relating to information systems. It is designed to fulfil the needs of the growing number of courses on, and interest in, computing and information systems which do not focus on the purely technological aspects, but seek to relate to business and organizational context.

Implementing Decision Support Systems: Methods, Techniques, and Tools

Ananth Srinivasan
University of Auckland

David Sundaram
University of Auckland

Joseph Davis
University of Wollongong

THE McGRAW-HILL COMPANIES

London · Burr Ridge IL · New York · St Louis · San Francisco · Auckland
Bogotá · Caracas · Lisbon · Madrid · Mexico · Milan
Montreal · New Delhi · Panama · Paris · San Juan · São Paulo
Singapore · Sydney · Tokyo · Toronto

Published by
McGraw-Hill Publishing Company
SHOPPENHANGERS ROAD, MAIDENHEAD, BERKSHIRE SL6 2QL, ENGLAND
Telephone +44 (0) 1628 502500
Fax: +44 (0) 1628 770224   Web site: http://www.mcgraw-hill. co.uk

---

British Library Cataloguing in Publication Data
A catalogue record for this book is available from the British Library

ISBN 007 7095081

Library of Congress Cataloguing-in-Publication Data
The LOC data for this book has been applied for and may be obtained from the Library of Congress, Washington, D.C.

Access, Excel, MSQuery, SQL Server 7, ODBC, and OLEDB are registered trademarks of Microsoft Corporation. Informix Dynamic Server (Universal Data Option), Visionary, and Schema Knowledge are registered trademarks of Informix Corporation. Clementine is a registered trademark of Integral Solutions Limited. SPSS is a registered trademark of SPSS, Inc.

Further information on this and other McGraw-Hill titles is to be found at
http://www.mcgraw-hill.co.uk
Author's website address:
http://www.mcgraw-hill.co.uk/textbooks/srinivasan

Sponsoring Editor: Elizabeth Robinson
Produced by: Steven Gardiner Ltd
Cover by: Hybert Design

McGraw-Hill

A Division of The McGraw·Hill Companies

5 4 3 2 1 CUP 4 3 2 1 0

Printed in Great Britain at the University Press, Cambridge

Contents

Preface

There are two key motivators for this book. First, a need felt and expressed by managers and decision support systems (DSS) designers for a book with a problem focus coupled with an implementation orientation. A book that went beyond DSS concepts in the abstract and clearly showed how to go about translating the concepts into design artefacts seemed to be wanting. Second, our observation that most of our acquaintances involved in teaching the topic of *Decision Support Systems* relied substantially on an experiential component to the course. In a typical course, students are engaged in combining lecture materials with hands-on exercises that necessitate the exploration of new information technologies and their application to particular problems of interest. While several useful books exist for the traditional aspects of delivery of the course, the experiential component meant that a substantial amount of implementation-oriented material had to be put together in a customised fashion. This involves finding design-oriented discussions from a variety of sources and presenting them to students in a manner that fits with a typical course to enable them to pursue the material on their own. Hence, we set out to produce a book on the topic that had an implementation focus that would address the needs of managers and DSS builders as well as lend itself to courses that relied on an experiential component.

The challenge of writing a book with such a focus in the area of information technology is accentuated because of the dynamic nature of the technology. New software platforms tend to proliferate and only some of them have the ability to retain a presence in the marketplace over a reasonable amount of time. When we started on this project, it was clear to us that we needed to combine the idea that certain implementation issues in the area of DSS were relatively abstract with the concern that implementation examples could only be discussed in the context of specific software platforms. These seemingly conflicting issues were dealt with by proposing an implementation framework that focused on *design capabilities* and discussing implementation examples that relied on *representative software platforms* that are able to deliver those capabilities. The examples used throughout the book rely on software that currently exist, are commercially available and run on standard hardware platforms. They highlight the application of essential DSS design capabilities in a way that the reader can gain familiarity with the ideas in a practical manner and is able to apply it to a class of software that exhibits comparable features.

The fundamental capabilities that we discuss in the book as essential for any good DSS design have to do with representing problems and manipulating represented objects with certain core ingredients: data, models, procedures and the delivery interface. The literature in the area has convincingly made the case for these core ingredients in DSS applications. Their identification, while important, is not novel. The real challenge lies in our ability to put them within an implementation context using specific software tools in a systematic manner. Our choice of software was guided by the dual concern of building on familiar platforms and introducing powerful capabilities that are found in emerging technologies.

Students of the subject usually come with a variety of backgrounds that touch on a subset of the core concepts of DSS design. For example, they may have a fair bit of experience in data management but very little in terms of modelling (or vice versa). We have dealt with this issue by presenting the core concepts in a framework that allows readers to locate their experiences within a coherent DSS design context. Data management, as it applies to DSS design, is one important piece of the overall puzzle and it must resonate with other design components. Similarly, building models must take into account the fact that input to and output from them must be integrated with an underlying data-management facility. Both these features must be made accessible to users in convenient forms. The glue that holds these activities together must be the problem-solving focus that guides design. Engaging in system design is done for the purpose of addressing tasks that are often complex. Throughout the book, we have tried to maintain this perspective on a problem (task) driven approach.

The reader should absorb the material presented here using the following simple set of questions as a guide:

- What is the overall problem that I am trying to support through the design of a system?
- How do I represent aspects of the problem in my design?
- What are some specific questions, the answers to which will help in addressing the problem?
- How do I answer questions of interest using my design?

The flow should be from a problem to its design using a set of appropriate tools and the consequent use of the design product. The book is not meant to be a tutorial on how to use a set of certain software packages. It is intended to provide a practical introduction to the use of software to assist in problem solving.

We emphasise the point that the specific software packages that we have highlighted in our examples are representatives of particular *classes* of software. For each package that the reader encounters in the book, there are several others in that class. Therefore, while the syntax of their use in the examples are relevant to show how they work, the principles that underlie their use must be transferable to other packages in that class. Readers should digest the material with a view of applying concepts using appropriate software and not necessarily only those that are discussed here.

Many of our academic colleagues in the US, Europe, New Zealand and Australia have contributed to our thinking about the topic. Feedback from our students over the years have helped a great deal in encouraging us to focus on implementation and design. We acknowledge their contribution. Thanks are also due to Elizabeth Robinson at McGraw Hill for her constant encouragement throughout the writing process.

The book is supported by a website www.mcgraw-hill.co.uk/textbooks/srinivasan which will support readers, in general, and instructors and students, in particular, who use this book in their courses. Many of the examples found in the book will have a more dynamic presentation on the website. Feedback from readers of the book and people browsing the website is welcomed. We hope that this book fills a need for those interested in the design and implementation aspects of this important topic.

Auckland, February 2000

Series Foreword

The Information Systems Series is a series of student and postgraduate texts covering a wide variety of topics relating to information systems. The focus of the series is the use of computers and the flow of information in business and large organisations. The series is designed to fill the needs of a growing number of courses on information systems and computing which do not focus on purely technical aspects but rather which seek to relate information systems to their commercial and organisational context.

The term 'information systems' has been defined as the effective design, delivery, use and impact of information technology in organisations and society. Utilising this broad definition it is clear that the subject is interdisciplinary. Thus the series seeks to integrate technological disciplines with management and other disciplines, for example, psychology and sociology. These areas do not have a natural home and were, until comparatively recently, rarely represented by single departments in universities and colleges. To put such books in a purely computer science or management series restricts potential readership and the benefits that such texts can provide. The series on information systems provides such a home.

The titles are mainly for student use, although certain topics will be covered at greater depth and be more research-oriented for postgraduate study.

The series includes the following areas, although this is not an exhaustive list: information systems development methodologies, office information systems, management information systems, decision support systems, information modelling and databases, systems theory, human aspects and the human-computer interface, application systems, technology strategy, planning and control, expert systems, knowledge acquisition and its representation.

A mention of the books so far published in the series gives a 'flavour' of the richness of the information systems series world. *Information and Data Modelling*, second edition (David Benyon) concerns itself with one very important aspect, the world of data, in some depth; *Information Systems Development: A Database Approach*, second edition (David Avison) provides a coherent methodology which has been widely used to develop adaptable computer systems using databases; *Business Management and Systems Analysis* (Eddie Moynihan) explores the areas of overlap between business and IT; *Information Systems: An Emerging Discipline?* (John Mingers and Frank Stowell – Editors) debates the practical and philosophical dimensions of the field; *Why Information Systems Fail* (Chris Sauer) looks at the reasons for IS failure and the problems of developing IS in organisations; *Human Computer Factors* (Andy Smith) emphasises user-centred design, usability and the role of the users; *Transforming the Business: The IT Contribution* (Robert Moreton and Myrvin Chester) discusses the role that IS/IT can play in organisational change; and the second edition of *Information Systems Development: Methodologies, Techniques and Tools* (David Avison and Guy Fitzgerald) provides a comprehensive coverage of the different elements of information systems development.

The Information Systems Lifecycle: A First Course in Information Systems (David Avison and Hanifa Shah) covers the basic material necessary in a first course in information systems. It can be used as a 'prequel' to Avison and Fitzgerald but can also be used 'stand-alone' where the teaching of IS does not go beyond a first course. The most recent additions to the series are *Rapid Information Systems Development* (Simon Bell and Trevor Wood-Harper) in which this area is explored with the help of many examples exploring real-world problems; and *Business Information Systems: A Process Approach* (Brian Warboys, Peter Kawalek, Ian Robertson and Mark Greenwood) which discusses how software support relates to business goals and hence increases the effectiveness of organisations.

We now welcome Ananath Srinivasan, David Sundaram and Joseph Davis' addition to the series. Decision-support systems remain an essential and exciting part of information systems in organisations, and in their book this very wide area – covering data and mathematical modelling, use of software tools, design, human cognition, the nature of decisions and many other topics – is described with copious real-world examples and cases which bring the material to life. This text will make an ideal base for a course in decision support systems.

David Avison
Guy Fitzgerald

1
Assisting Organisational Problem Solving

1.1 Introduction

The term Decision Support Systems (DSS) has been widely used to refer to systems that are computer-based aids for decision making. Over the years, the term has come to refer to systems that can lend support to decision makers involved in solving problems of some complexity. This is done by identifying and representing important aspects of a problem in a form that is amenable to the application of computer-based manipulation. In other words, we consider how the problem can first be described in a particular software environment and then subjected to transformations that give us insights about the problem under consideration. Such systems may be large shared designs involving multiple users scattered across a computer network. Alternatively, they could be single-user desktop systems that are entirely under the control of individual problem solvers in an organisation. Today's technology offers ample scope for both approaches (and anything in-between) to the design of such systems. An important implication of the DSS idea is that decision makers often engage in *ad-hoc problem solving*. What this means is that a resolution of a problem is often obtained by the *exploration of data*. This capability is at least as crucial as the implementation of predetermined methods of solution to a particular task. Effective DSS design then is a process that leverages information technology to support organisational problem solving. This is done by producing design artefacts that are linked to problems and tasks that individuals face. The design process must recognise the nature of the tasks that it seeks to support and translate that to the systematic and targeted application of information concepts and technologies that explicitly address those tasks. The link between specific organisational problems (and tasks) and relevant supporting computer-based design products is at the heart of this book. To summarise the discussion, the important considerations are as follows.

1. An organisation provides a context in which problems have to be addressed. Decision making is essentially the consequence of addressing these problems.
2. Problems can be detailed by identifying specific tasks that suggest action.
3. Problems can be represented in a form that is conducive to providing computer-based support for decision making. This is the heart of application design.
4. Tasks can be addressed by using the design product on an ongoing basis.

A useful place to start thinking about the *design process* is to ask the following question: Are there some general concepts that can be brought to bear on the issue of designing such systems? A well-accepted starting point to address this question lies in the exploration of the general capabilities that are essential for good DSS design. Three important guiding concepts help us in clarifying how to proceed.

- The essence of problems and tasks can be captured by focusing on data aspects that best describe them. Hence, systems need the capability to manage large volumes of *data*.

```
┌─────────────────────────────────────────┐  ┌─────────────────────────────────────────┐
│ Data management                           │  │ Data manipulation                         │
│                                           │  │                                           │
│ ● Can we identify important data elements │  │ ● Can we identify specific tasks that     │
│   that are central to the problem?        │  │   require data to be transformed in       │
│ ● How is the data going to be collected   │  │   specific ways?                          │
│   and main-tained?                        │  │ ● Can we classify these transformation    │
│ ● What is the data organisation strategy? │  │   methods as being simple or complex?     │
│ ● Can we think of specific data retrieval │  │ ● What is the system organisation         │
│   requests that users may want answers    │  │   strategy for keeping track of these     │
│   for?                                    │  │   methods?                                │
└─────────────────────────────────────────┘  └─────────────────────────────────────────┘

┌───────────────────────────────────────────────────────────────────────────────────────┐
│ The problem solver                                                                        │
│                                                                                           │
│ ● How does the user interact with the system?                                             │
│ ● How does the user specify a request that needs a specific subset of data from the       │
│   dataset?                                                                                 │
│ ● How does the user specify the interaction between certain data manipulation rules and   │
│   subsets of data?                                                                         │
│ ● How does the user specify the manner in which the results of a particular request are   │
│   displayed?                                                                               │
└───────────────────────────────────────────────────────────────────────────────────────┘
```

Figure 1.1. Critical aspects of DSS design.

This means that data about the task environment must be gathered systematically and maintained in a fashion that yields relevant answers in response to targeted questions. Such data management must be conducted in an efficient fashion.

● We gain insights about problems by looking at data from a variety of perspectives. Often such insights are gained by appropriately manipulating or transforming data that we gather. Hence, the ability to maintain specific data-manipulation rules is essential. A typical example of what we mean by this is a *model* that takes as input those data that describe essential aspects of a task (e.g. product costs and demands) and manipulates it as per specified rules (a solution method or an *algorithm*) in order to produce a useful result (e.g. an indication of how much of the product should be produced each month). Usually, several such models need to be maintained as part of the system. Furthermore, the ability to add new models as needs arise is essential.

● A well designed system is useful only to the extent that individuals can put the system to work in a relatively straightforward manner. Users of these systems need the capability of accessing data from the database and specifying the *interaction* between such data and one or more of the above-mentioned models in a manner that is easy to use.

Figure 1.1 captures the essentials of how we think about DSS design in this book. Such design guidelines are only useful to the extent that relevant computer technologies are brought to bear on specific organisational problems in a systematic manner. An example of an organisational task situation requiring information-technology-based support will be useful in clarifying some of these ideas. We describe such a situation next.

1.1.1 An Example: Evaluating Potential Customers in the Financial-services Industry (Labe, 1994)

Merrill Lynch, an international full-service brokerage provider, was faced with the issue of identifying and attracting clients for whom it would provide advice on managing and building their financial assets. In an attempt to increase their client base, the main strategy was to identify potential customers who are most likely to fit a desirable profile from the perspective of the company. Several data options were available for pursuing this. These ranged from examining publicly available data regarding such things as household income and socioeconomic classification groups to more detailed, and relatively difficult to obtain, data at the level of individual households, such as family income, occupation, vehicle ownership, etc.

The approach that was followed was to generate a database that consisted of a mix of existing and known Merrill Lynch clients who fit a profile deemed to be desirable, and a set of randomly chosen households. Demographic data, considered to be relevant for the purposes of evaluating potential and existing customers, was obtained from third-party sources. The objective, from a decision-making point of view at this stage, was to examine the data and possibly identify those demographic characteristics that define an individual as a client that the organisation would like to have. If such an understanding could be obtained, then the assessment of a potential client could be done efficiently, thereby increasing the likelihood of the client base growing.

The critical issue here was the identification of client characteristics: What makes a person a likely client? How does one systematically sift through demographic data and find out what the important and determining characteristics are? In order to do this, a statistical approach known as discriminant analysis was used. The technique essentially capitalises on the knowledge about whether an individual belongs to a particular category or not: in this case, individuals who were existing Merrill Lynch clients were classified as belonging to one category which identified desirable characteristics. Individuals chosen randomly (from a third-party database) were classified as belonging to a 'non-priority' category. Discriminant analysis uses a statistical model that identifies those variables (demographic data in this case) that are most influential in correctly placing individuals in one of the two categories. An added benefit of the technique is that it provides a quantitative measure of how much importance (the weight) should be assigned to each of these variables. This addresses the question of how much more influential one variable is (e.g. household income) over another (e.g. vehicle ownership) in classifying a person as belonging to one or the other of the two groups. What this enabled the modeller to do was to use this information to evaluate a prospective client by computing a score based on the demographic profile of the individual and the weights provided by the discriminant analysis. This score could then be used to say whether there was a reasonable likelihood that an individual would be a client that Merrill Lynch would like to have or not.

The discriminant analysis model was used on the dataset described above to first obtain information that could be used to evaluate clients. If a prospective client was placed in the priority category by the model, then resources were devoted to marketing the services to these individuals. Results showed that this approach was successful in obtaining significant growth in the client base. The design of an application that combined relevant data with useful models resulted in having an impact on the basic issue of obtaining growth in the client base.

A number of interesting observations can be made about this problem-solving situation and its implications for DSS design.

1. *The Task Situation:* The objective here was to find a target population in order to market a particular set of financial services. The problem was approached by first understanding the characteristics of a desirable target population. The problem solving strategy was to then apply this knowledge to prospective clients.
2. *The Data Implications:* Data about existing customers was readily available within the organisation. Data about individuals who were not current customers and some demographic data were obtained from a third party.

3. *The Modelling Implications:* A statistical model was used in order to extract useful information in the context of the current problem. The model was able to use the data about customers in order to highlight, in a quantitative manner, which characteristics of individuals were important to consider.
4. *Solution Strategy:* The information about important characteristics was then applied to potential customers to sort them into the target population. The target population thus defined then formed a dataset used for further promotion of services by the organisation.

The example highlights many important aspects of successful DSS applications. The appropriate interaction between data and models clearly emerges in this case as instrumental in dealing with the problem at hand. However, for this to happen, the data needs to be managed and provided to a modelling environment in order for useful information to emerge. A number of potential issues that have not been explicitly addressed in the example could be explored by the reader.

- The customer (existing and potential) database could be a useful resource for other parts of the organisation in addition to addressing the immediate needs for marketing new services.
- A systematic approach to maintaining and using models could be addressed so that the customer database could provide input for additional problem-solving tasks.
- The design of a system that leverages customer information could address issues of data access to a wide community of users at varying skill levels.
- The system could be a useful tool for repeatedly identifying potential customers on a periodic basis or for exploring new ways of utilising customer data.

1.2 The Scope of This Book

Several conceptual and abstract pieces that talk about building decision support systems exist in the literature. However, it is equally important that guidelines for the systematic design and development of such systems be explored, described and debated. It is critical that we examine particular examples of successful DSS implementations with a view towards asking the following question: How can we generalise from these experiences to understand the design process better? Further, with the proliferation of powerful desktop-design tools that are now available, the time is right to explore how the design of such systems may be brought well within the scope of individual decision makers.

Our objective in this book is twofold. First, we want to explore what the current concepts and trends are in making the design of such systems feasible. Second, we want to explore some technologies that make the implementation of these concepts possible. In order for such an approach to be successful three issues need to be addressed. First, what are some of the well-accepted concepts that may be powerful and stable principles behind the design of these systems. Second, what are the design tools that are available *today* that may be incorporated in the design of these systems. Third, what are some examples of typical systems that combine the concepts with the tools. We want this book to serve as a guide to potential decision makers in organisations to think about situations where information technologies could serve as powerful aids to problem solving. It is also important that the book serve as a *practical guide* to decision makers, designers and students of the area. By including concrete examples of developed systems, we want readers to develop a sense of assurance – that it is possible to build powerful systems that deal with non-trivial problems using affordable and widely available design tools.

In this chapter, we explore a few more examples of decision support applications. We do this in order to weave into the discussion some of the concepts about organisational decision making and applications design that we have introduced thus far. Learning by example is perhaps the most powerful way to explore new ideas in this discipline. We try to encourage our readers to relate concepts and ideas to concrete examples in this chapter and throughout the book. The important issues that permeate these examples and are discussed explicity later in this chapter address the following issues:

- What are the essential characteristics of the problem that need support?
- What specific tasks need to be addressed in this context?
- What are the data aspects of the problem that can be captured in a convenient form?
- How is the data manipulated to address the tasks?
- What software platforms could help us in describing the problem adequately and addressing specific tasks?
- Are there some design guidelines that could be useful in building a system?
- How does the user interact with the system?

While not all these issues are explicitly highlighted in each of the examples, they certainly warrant some thought and discussion.

1.3 Key Concepts for Decision Support

What are some of the essential concepts and ideas that are critical for the design of decision support systems? In order to answer this question meaningfully, we need to examine what the elements of the design process are. Earlier, we talked about data and models as essential components of the system and the need for the user to have a mechanism for the specification of exchange between the database and the model base. This idea needs some clarification.

1.3.1 The Roles of Data and Models

If data and models are essential ingredients of a system, a paramount issue is one of representing them in the design, For example, when we think about data, a commonly utilised means of representation is to use table structures (in the relational database sense). Many widely used systems for managing data today utilise this approach. Consequently, a typical data-intensive application consists of several tables containing data that together constitute the database for that application. Another commonly recognised approach to representing data is a spreadsheet. Many financial applications, for example, use the familiar columns-and-rows approach for encoding data that describe a particular application.

The issue of models is a little more complicated. If we consider a model to be a collection of data-manipulation rules, models run the gamut from quite simple (e.g. one that calculates an average of series of numbers – a statistical model – or a future value of an annuity – a financial model) to the quite complex (e.g. the optimised values of decision variables in a mathematical programming problem). In either case, the model is characterised by the application of a dataset as input to the model resulting in another dataset that we consider to be the manipulation result. Often, the simpler (and more predictable) model types are incorporated as part of a representation framework. For example, we see statistical and financial functions built into database and spreadsheet environments as a matter of course. More complicated models need specialised tools for their representation. For example, an optimisation algorithm applied to large problems is probably best represented using a programming language. The question is how can such a representation coexist with other models written with a different set of tools, and with a dataset with which it interacts?

1.3.1.1 An Example: Managing Supplier–Distributor Relationships in a Volatile Business Environment (Blakely and Evans, 1985)

A high-technology firm was interested in managing its supplier relationships in a business environment characterised by a high degree of volatility. Specifically, the firm was engaged in negotiations with international suppliers for products and components that had a volatile demand pattern and short life cycles. When the firm was negotiating with a particular supplier, it was important to understand the financial implications of different business conditions on cash flow and profitability of the firm. For example, an upsurge in the demand for a product might place a cash-flow strain on the firm. On the other hand, dealing with such cash-flow considerations by reducing the volume of trade might result in lower revenues because of reduced market share. The key negotiating points for the firm are the purchase price of products from the suppliers and the payment terms. Decision makers saw this as a situation involving a trade-off between these two factors. They were prepared to agree to a higher purchase price if that meant easier payment terms. This might be beneficial in a situation where the expected demand for their products was increasing rapidly – a situation that often occurs in the high-technology sector with new products. However, if business conditions changed so that demand for the product levelled off, the cash-flow situation would not be critical and price concessions would not be advisable. What management required was a tool that could be used interactively in a negotiation situation with suppliers where different business conditions could be dynamically modelled. The information that was required was a clear indication of the impact of different purchase price and payment terms on profitability and cash flow.

The modellers approached the problem as one of (a) modelling the business conditions faced by the firm and (b) displaying the data graphically and in tabular form on an as-needed basis and (c) encouraging the exploration of various business scenarios dynamically to understand the impact of a particular set of negotiation conditions.

The data necessary for the modelling task involved standard accounting entities such as purchase and selling prices, costs, accounts payables and receivables, working capital, profits and return on assets. Model parameters included sales-growth rates, price-erosion rates, payables and receivables lags, and cost of capital. Values for these parameters could be input into the system as problem assumptions that could be dynamically adjusted to investigate alternative business scenarios. The relationships between the basic accounting entities were modelled as algebraic expressions in a spreadsheet-like environment.

The results of interest involved profitability and cash-flow figures for different values of purchase price and payment lags. By allowing these results to be displayed on a graph, the user could readily see these impacts on performance. Furthermore, the utility of the system was greatly enhanced by allowing the display of purchase price and payment-lag combinations to maintain a specific cash flow or profitability level, emphasising the trade-off involved between the critical variables.

In this example, accurately modelling the problem and displaying the results in an intuitively understandable manner were the essential design ingredients. In contrast to the earlier example where the database (of customers) was a significant element of the application, here the collection of expressions which could be used to dynamically evaluate the financial consequences of changing assumptions was the key. The example underscores the importance of scenario analysis as a critical component of decision making. Many decision support applications need to support the user's ability to explore and evaluate alternative solutions dynamically in order to be of real value. The questions asked earlier about the task situation, the data and modelling implications, and the solution strategy need to be applied to this example as well in order to fully appreciate the design implications.

Problem representations are just the first step with decision support applications. The reason why we seek to represent problems with all the complexity implied by them is in order to enable us as decision makers to address ongoing tasks with reference to the representations. For example, a general problem of allocating financial resources to a portfolio of investment options with specified performance objectives may be represented adequately by a particular model. The associated dataset containing data about economic parameters, multiple investors, etc. is a snapshot of the problem at a particular instant (an instantiation of the problem). Clearly, the dataset could change over time since some investors may drop out, new ones may enter and economic parameters change over time. The underlying model remains the same; it is the dataset that interacts with the model that changes over time to reflect changes in the problem environment. Furthermore, as decision makers, we may be interested in applying the model to some subset of the data as opposed to the entire dataset (e.g. applying the model to a particular investor). The message here is that the decision maker's activity is defined in terms of specific tasks over time. Execution of these tasks involves the specification of an interaction between (part or the whole of) the dataset and one or more models. Some of these interactions may be predictable, such as the generation of monthly statements for the investor. Others might be defined on an ad-hoc basis as the need arises. In either case, what is called for is the ability to deal with tasks by manipulating the representation of the problem. This could involve something as simple as retrieving data based on some criterion ('Display high performing investments in the month of May') or something a little more complicated as the production of an optimal result obtained by applying a dataset to a model ('Display the optimal dollar amounts to invest in each of five investment options').

We conclude this section with some clarification about the nature of decision making in this environment as we see it. We view computer-based decision support as an environment that enables problems to be represented adequately. Further, decision making is viewed as an activity that an individual engages in on an ongoing basis in response to specific situations. In a computer-based environment, such activity translates into task definitions that are then addressed against represented problems. Such activity may be pre-planned and periodic or it may be ad hoc in nature. In either case, a good decision support system should enable a satisfactory method of dealing with the particular task at hand.

1.3.2 Decision Making

A brief discussion about the nature of decision making will clarify the context in which we propose that these systems should be designed. There are a number of concepts and theories that have examined organisational decision making. Many of these are reviewed in the next chapter. However, it is useful, through an example, to emphasise aspects of decision making that make the consideration of designing information support a worthwhile exercise.

1.3.2.1 *An Example: Managing Customers in the Mobile-phone Market* (SmarTone, 1999)

SmarTone is a Hong Kong-based organisation that provides digital mobile telecommu-
nication services to about half a million customers handling about two million calls every
day. Paralleling the experience of mobile-phone services all over the world, customers
increasingly have an array of choices in terms of service providers. The situation is further
complicated by the mandate of the Hong Kong government that stipulates that customers
must be able to keep a single mobile-phone number even if they switch service providers.
SmarTone is faced with the dual problem of retaining existing customers and attracting
new customers in the face of a growing and fiercely competitive market.

The organisation's strategy to deal with this issue is to take the view that data about
customers and their usage patterns must be systematically collected, managed and
analysed in order to continue its leadership in the mobile-phone-services marketplace.
The sheer volume of data, and the promise of the volume expanding at an increasing rate,
led the organisation to utilise a data-warehousing approach. The solution should be able
to provide acceptable performance with the current volume of data and, furthermore,
must be scalable to deal with the future data needs of the organisation.

The organisation plans to systematically collect data about each of their customers and
their calling patterns in order to better understand their usage behaviour. For existing
customers, the retention of SmarTone as their service provider could be made attractive by
creating services that offer greater value based on need. Such services may be financial or
technical, or both. In order to attract new customers, the data warehouse must be mined in
order to extract information that would be useful for the creation of new targeted
programmes that would be appealing to them. After a careful evaluation of existing
technologies, the organisation decided on implementing a data-warehousing solution
using the Informix Dynamic Server.

In explaining its choice, the organisation stressed that the importance of the issue to the
organisation and the size of the problem were critical to their implementation strategy.
The data-warehouse approach would serve as the foundation in which potentially useful
data would be housed. This would then serve as a base from which useful information
needs to be mined, using appropriate tools, to provide input into the market-development
issues outlined earlier. In order for the solution to work, the technology that supports it
must be:

- efficient in terms of its ability to search a large volume of data and retrieve specific
  subsets;
- flexible to deal with changing user perspectives about the data;
- scalable to cope with a rapidly expanding database.

With the implementation in place, it will now be up to the organisation to make the best
use of the available data by designing appropriate methods by which useful information
may be extracted over time.

Considering the decision-making tasks involved in this example, there clearly is no one
correct solution to the set of problems faced by this organisation. A possible solution
strategy can only be formulated by exploration of the data to understand what their
customers have actually been doing. The data that describe this exist; however, an
interpretation of the data, after some analysis, is what is required to consider how best
to proceed. Such an analysis can be facilitated by the system solution that has been
implemented. But the issue of how to analyse the data and what alternatives to explore
characterises the decision-making process. It must consist of making assumptions about

the environment that the organisation operates in and testing the sensitivity of changes of those assumptions to the resulting dataset. The example underscores the ad-hoc nature of decision making where the system can provide some support; it is up to the decision maker to make the best use of what the system can provide.

1.3.3 Design Tools – the Landscape

In this section, we provide a brief survey of some important design tools that have made it possible for us to implement powerful decision support concepts. We are not saying that all of these platforms will be necessary for the good design of any system. However, collectively they offer a rich set of capabilities. An understanding of what they do will allow an individual to make informed choices during design to best serve the needs of the application. The choice of the tools is particularly important since we want to discuss tools that are widely available and are well supported. An important objective of this book is to encourage a wide array of individuals to seriously consider doing developmental work themselves. A prerequisite for this is the availability of powerful design tools.

- *Relational Databases:* If datasets constitute an important component of decision support systems, then a mechanism for managing data is an important design tool. Relational database technology is a well recognised and widely available data-management tool. Relational database systems enable efficient storage and retrieval of data and offer a variety of convenient modules that can be used for developing data-intensive applications.
- *Spreadsheets:* The popularity of spreadsheet systems has been unrivalled in the brief history of software packages. They provide an intuitive manner in which problems can be represented, namely the familiar columns-and-rows format. Many spreadsheet systems available today have sophisticated capabilities that allow the specification of models of varying degrees of complexity and graphics for the display of information.
- *Programming Languages:* When models get complex, it is sometimes necessary to rely on special-purpose languages for their specification. The built-in facilities of spreadsheet systems, for example, are not powerful enough for specifying a complex set of data-manipulation rules. Often one finds special-purpose models written in a programming language like C which is available in the public domain. Increasingly, the object-oriented approach to programming has become a valuable tool for systems development and its widespread use cannot be ignored. It is essential that well-designed decision support systems have the capability to utilise models written in such language environments.
- *Object Relational Systems:* These systems combine the data-handling capabilities of a relational database systems with the detailed specification capabilities of a programming language. The net effect is a single development environment which allows the simultaneous specification and handling of datasets and models of seemingly arbitrary complexity. This capability is particularly well suited for the design of decision support systems, given that the ability to manage datasets and to specify models are central to their proper functioning.
- *On-line Analytical Processing Systems:* An important aspect of decision support systems is its ability to support ad-hoc investigation by the user. This implies that it is impossible to predict how a user is going to specify a subset of the data for inspection. On-line Analytical Processing (OLAP) systems are design tools that make it easy for the specification and retrieval of data based on a wide range of criteria. The power that OLAP systems have over traditional relational database systems lies in their ability to

represent data in a manner that allows the efficient and accurate processing of arbitrarily specified retrieval criteria.

- *Data Warehouses:* Increasingly, the concept of a repository for large amounts of data has been put forward as a useful way to organise data for unspecified utility in the future. The idea behind data warehousing is that tools that capture and store data in an organised manner are essential to support future decision making. Unlike traditional database management, which typically engages in a process to identify data objects of *current interest* in the organisation, data warehousing takes a broader view of the temporal dimension. Tools that allow such data stores to be automatically examined for interesting relationships between datasets are particularly useful in this context. The area of data mining has become one of the most useful decision support techniques available today. This approach is well suited for the notion of ad-hoc decision making which is key to good decision support systems.

- *Interface and Integration Tools:* Many of the tools mentioned above provide convenient easy-to-use mechanisms that allow a user to interact with the system. For example, popular database systems provide the capability to develop forms and reports that enable users to conveniently enter and retrieve data. With decision support systems, however, there is a need for modular development and integration. This means that a complete system may be designed from multiple tools. The problem that this presents is twofold. First, how are users going to refer to these multiple components of a system in a seamless manner? Second, how are the various components going to exchange data amongst themselves? An investigation of these issues is clearly important in the context of the applications that we refer to in this book.

1.3.4 Modularity and Integration

The preceding section implies that there is a variety of capabilities that can contribute to the design of a single application. The specific capabilities that are actually used in an application will naturally depend on the essential nature of the problem that is being supported. In some cases, it may be necessary to build an application by integrating diverse capabilities under a single umbrella. A useful approach for dealing with this issue is to consider designing parts of the application in a modular independent fashion and integrating the completed modules appropriately as the final design step. This is a powerful concept which finds an important application in DSS implementation, especially as it relates to ad-hoc problem solving using the system. The approach we propose in this book emphasises built-in flexibility whereby the user can have access to multiple models of the decision problem and multiple solvers to each of the models. The ability to link the appropriate representations of the problem with the relevant datasets and solvers is a critical capability that must be supported. Probably the most effective means to achieve this is to instantiate problem-solving scenarios for each new situation by integrating the appropriate modules of data, models and solvers. For certain complex problems, the support may involve multiple models that need to be integrated in complex ways. Consistent with the principles of object orientation, the key idea is that the complexity of the decision support-system design can be better handled with the concept of dynamic integration of appropriate modules, be they data, models or solvers.

1.3.4.1 *An Example: Understanding the Effects of Promotion in Retail Marketing* (Davis and Sundaram, 1995)

Retail marketing is an area that is highly dependent on promotion and advertising.

Intensively competitive retail sectors are often characterised by large volume and low profit margins. A good example of this sector is the grocery-chain industry. This example describes a system that was designed to address decision support needs of a specific manufacturer of products sold through grocery-store chains in Australasia. This retail sector is one where the promotion and advertising of products can have a significant impact on sales volumes and profit margins. However, promotion-related expenditures have to be judiciously used so that the returns are measurable and justify such expenditure. The problem faced by a particular manufacturer of grocery-store items was to understand the relationship between in-store promotion of specific products and the associated sales of those products. In particular, this information was useful in negotiating with the retailers the cost of these promotions to the manufacturer.

The manufacturer sells a variety of products through several grocery-chain stores. Sales data at the level of individual products is systematically tracked by the manufacturer. Furthermore, data about the sales of products by other manufacturers is available from a third party which collects and manages this data. Retail-store products may be promoted in a variety of different ways. For example, in-store coupons, displayed in bins at the end of the aisles and checkout-counter displays, are all available options for promotion. Each promotion type has an associated cost to the manufacturer. All sales and promotion data per product are available over a specified period of time.

The questions faced by individuals involved in promotion-related decision making include:

- Which specific products should be chosen for promotion in a specified time window?
- In which retail stores should the promotions be conducted?
- What types of promotions would be most effective (likely to result in increased sales) for specific combinations of products and retail stores?
- What is the optimal level of spending for each promotion instance?

In this situation, the decision modellers were confronted with a substantial amount of product sales and promotion data at the store level. This was helpful to track trends in sales and promotion since the data was time specific. The issue of understanding the nature of the relationship between promotion and sales was a little more difficult. Several quantitative models that mathematically describe the relationship between these two variables exist in the literature. The challenge facing the modellers was to be able to make sense of the large volume of data, select a subset of interest from it and then see how promotion levels affect sales.

The data was managed by a relational database management system. Typical database queries were used to isolate product and promotion combinations of interest; for example, a rank-ordered list of all products by sales volume with associated promotion expenditures over the past 4-week time period. The mathematical model was then applied to the subset by using a spreadsheet environment. The data of interest was linked to a spreadsheet where the model was defined. Certain parameters of the model could be adjusted by the user to do a sensitivity-type analysis with the data. The spreadsheet also enabled a graphical display of the relationship between promotion and sales so that the user could obtain instant visual feedback about the nature of the relationship under changing circumstances. Most important, given a set of parameter values that described a particular scenario, the quantity of sales of a particular product corresponding to any level of expenditure of a particular promotion type was available to the user. This was valuable information that could serve as the basis for making promotion-related decisions.

This example emphasised the importance of modularity of design. There was a data aspect to the problem that was handled in a traditional database environment. There was a quantitative modelling aspect to the problem that was handled in a spreadsheet environment. Integrating links between objects in the two environments allowed for the application of the models to relevant subsets of the data. However, the modular approach allowed users to conduct analysis, make changes or process queries in any one of the modules on an as-needed basis. We again suggest that readers apply the questions, asked of the earlier examples in this chapter, to clarify aspects of design that may be relevant.

1.3.5 Information Presentation

Given that users of DSSs are typically managerial personnel who tend to function against time constraints, the facility for inputting data and the presentation of information or results by the system should be such as to enable them to engage in a meaningful dialogue with the system as well as for interpreting the outputs quickly and effectively. This implies that the system should be easy to learn and use, unimpeded by constraining demands of the syntax and semantics of a complex user-interface system. Such a system has elements of both systematic provision of inputs by the user (action language) as well as the presentation and interpretation of the results (presentation language). The emergence of a new generation of powerful workstations with highly expressive graphical user interfaces (GUIs) and point-and-click input mechanisms have certainly contributed to improving the quality and efficacy of human–computer interaction. There is emerging evidence that graphical and visual means of presentation enables users to absorb the information and make better decisions. However, in the context of DSS, there are additional concerns relating to the following:

- *Consistency:* the 'look and feel' of the various layers of the user interface should be consistent,
- *Seamless Integration:* at the user-interface level moving across diverse user goals or aspects of the decision problem, models, solvers, etc. should be transparent to the user. It should not involve too many system-oriented complexities.

In the examples that we have seen in this chapter, there are some common threads pertaining to information access and presentation issues. In each case, there is the issue of linking selected data with models that manipulate them. In some cases, the models are more complex than others. In all cases, the way in which the results are presented to the user is critical. The use of graphical representations of results can be a very useful tool to visually convey the impact of changing problem definitions and assumptions. Finally, it is important to note that the components of the system must be integrated in a manner that allows users to exploit relationships between objects in these various components. Users must be able to use a common interface to point to these components and specify interactions in order to view results in a manner that is intuitive and relatively easy to use. Visualisation is now seen as an important design principle in the decision support arena. It is important to explore ways by which the power of visualisation can be integrated into the design of decision support applications.

1.4 The Approach Taken in This Book

The support of complex decision making using computer-based tools has a well-established tradition in the academic and practitioner literature. Over the last two decades, developments in hardware, software and the information-system infrastructure (the technological base) have motivated a wide array of concepts, applications and development tools. Today, we are at a stage where this landscape is not only complex; it is dynamic to a dizzying degree. Concepts that have firm theoretical and formal underpinnings lend a semblance of stability to this field. They are the foundations of successful applications and the development of design platforms that facilitate the construction of systems. However, improvements in the technological base have motivated innovations in the application of powerful concepts. For example, high speed publicly accessible networks have combined with powerful desktop workstations and graphical user interfaces to enable the implementation of applications involving shared information. The challenge that faces the information-system specialist is one of recognising stable and potentially useful conceptual ideas that drive application development, while sorting through the rapidly changing technological landscape to integrate those aspects of it that lend themselves to the effective implementation of those concepts. Our motivation in this book is to address this set of issues in the context of a well-defined class of problems. We will attempt to do this by first articulating the nature of the decision-making problem and then providing a possible implementation strategy utilising a *currently viable set of tools*. It is important to note that our approach is twofold: first, we want to highlight a set of concepts and principles that have the potential for addressing complex decision-making problems; second, we want to demonstrate the applicability of some well-understood yet current and widely accessible building blocks for implementing these concepts and principles. Surely the implementation approach will and must change over time as the technological base changes. However, if the underlying concepts have a solid foundation, they will stand the test of time and lend themselves to implementation, using evolving tools of design.

This book is about designing useful systems that are applicable to an important class of decision-making situations. However, it is meant to encourage the development of such systems by a wide variety of users and not just technical specialists. Consider the spreadsheet as a design tool. Today, it is a framework that is familiar to virtually all computer-system users. It is used for the *autonomous development* of applications ranging from the simple to the complex. It is now time to go beyond a single-development framework, like the spreadsheet, to include a wide array of tools. It is not as if the spreadsheet has become irrelevant. In fact, there is an array of tools, both software and hardware, that are competing for relevance with familiar paradigms such as the spreadsheet. We need a systematic way by which we can harness the potential of these multiple ways of thinking about designing systems.

A *roadmap* that provides a brief outline of the contents of the book will be useful to the reader at this stage. Bearing in mind that an important emphasis of this book is on designing systems with respect to decision making in organisations, the terrain that we cover in Chapter 2 introduces organisational decision making from a variety of different perspectives. This draws from the work of several streams of research that has since received wide acceptance by decision-making theorists and practitioners. Understanding decision making leads to the discussion of linked-design processes that are essential for the delivery of completed applications. The chapter emphasises concepts that relate to decision making since ultimately that is the activity that we seek to support through design. Readers of this book who come from a design background will find this material useful in placing design in an organisational context. Readers who are familiar with the literature on organisational decision making will find this chapter to be a useful review of important concepts, particularly as they apply to the design of applications.

Chapter 3 proposes a useful framework for discourse for the material covered in this book that relates conceptual-level task requirements with implementation-level design platforms. We then step through a collection of design technologies that are capable of delivering the capabilities that we seek in decision support applications. We do this by example to show the technical requirements and the manner in which they can be met. Note that many of these technologies are easy to find in today's commercial software environment. This chapter serves as a quick introduction to the major software platforms that are discussed in the later chapters. Readers with significant experience in the use of database technologies and spreadsheets may focus on the sections on object relational databases and visualisation technologies. These are relatively new software environments and have considerable potential for DSS applications. Readers without such a background may find it useful to sharpen their skills in the more basic areas covered in this chapter by expanding on the brief examples that are discussed.

Chapter 4 discusses the development and design of a specific application to meet the task requirements in a particular application domain. The example highlights the various aspects of the application as outlined in this chapter and the manner in which different technologies are brought to bear on the design solution in an integrated manner. Readers will find it useful to ask how they would have approached the design problem in this chapter. The chapter can also be read independently as a case study to understand the issues involved in linking the specific requirements of a particular organisational situation with modular design and integration.

Chapters 5, 6 and 7 cover three vital aspects of design that are essential for the successful implementation of decision support applications. They are object relational systems, visualisation and data warehousing, respectively. We focus on these aspects because of their functionality and ability to support the requirements as outlined in Chapter 3. In keeping with the spirit of the book, we focus on examples to demonstrate the utility of these platforms. Much of this material discusses relatively new technologies compared with those discussed in Chapter 4. To that extent, readers will want to spend considerable time trying to understand how these technologies are linked to specific task requirements. These chapters may offer some guidelines for the acquisition of specific software for pursuing design projects that use these capabilities.

Chapter 8 provides some concluding remarks about the material that we have covered here. Our intent is not to provide a treatise on normative design for decision support applications. Neither are we proposing to compile a compendium of software tools for building systems that we are interested in. Rather, by focusing on examples that cover a range of task complexities, relying on case studies and demonstrating the use of selected but powerful software tools, we aim to provide the reader with a basis for exploring the possibilities that exist for building useful systems.

References

Blakely, D. and Evans, S. (1985) Managing high technology supplier/distributor relationships, *DSS Transactions*.

Cattell, R. G. G. (1994) Object data management concepts, *Object Data Management: Object-Oriented and Extended Relational Database Systems*, Addison-Wesley Publishing Company.

Davis, J. G. and Sundaram, D. (1995) PETAPS: A prototype decision support system for consumer product marketing and promotion, *European Journal of Operational Research*, **87**, 247–256.

Labe, R. P. (1994) Database marketing increases prospecting effectiveness at Merrill Lynch, *Interfaces*, **24**(5), 1–12.

SmarTone builds one of Hong Kong's largest on-line data warehouses with Informix technology, 9 February 1999, Informix Press Release, Menlo Park, California.

Sprague, R. H. (1980) A framework for the development of DSS, *MIS Quarterly*, **4**(4).

DISCUSSION QUESTIONS

1. Define in your own words, what the essential features of a decision support application ought to be.
2. What are the key aspects of organisational decisions that such systems can support?
3. Describe a decision support situation of your choice and identify what the key problems and tasks are.
4. What are the some data and modelling aspects of the situation that you identified in #3?
5. Compare the four examples of the applications in this chapter in terms of typical decision support-system characteristics.

2
Decision Making in Organisations: Concepts and Design Implications

2.1 Introduction

A good understanding of the structure of organisational decisions and the process of decision making is an important prerequisite to building effective decision support systems (DSS). With this objective in mind, we will present a range of concepts and frameworks that pertain to both normative and descriptive models of decisions and the process of decision making. The discussion will also deal with diverse approaches to classifying decisions and the impacts of human cognitive limitations on decision making and performance. Some aspects of the organisational context as they bear on decision making will also be covered in this chapter.

It might appear intuitively obvious to us that in order to build effective computer systems to assist managers and other relevant organisational participants in decision making, we need to start with analysis of the specific tasks they perform and the important decisions they make. However, such an approach was not very common in the early years when information systems were first introduced in organisations. The design of these systems tended to be guided more by what could be done with the information that was *already available* rather than what information was *actually needed* for making better decisions (Simon, 1977). The consequence of this was a situation in which the design and implementation of information systems led to '... an over-abundance of irrelevant information' which rarely got used by managers (Ackoff, 1967). The voluminous reports produced by such systems (typically by processing large numbers of routine transactions) were largely ignored by managers. Many large management-information-system projects had to be abandoned. By the mid- to late 1960s, much of the early enthusiasm for computer-based information systems had evaporated.

Several developments around this time were to radically transform system design from the perspectives of both theory and practice. Perhaps one of the most crucial was the emergence and gradual acceptance of some seminal ideas and concepts on decision making in organisations. Another set of developments were essentially technological in nature. Innovations such as time sharing and on-line systems and database-management technology offered, for the first time, the promise of managers being able to work directly with computer systems rather than having to rely on hard-copy reports prepared by information-system analysts. These were soon to be followed by the rapid evolution and spread of personal workstations and computers with their easy-to-learn and use graphical user interfaces. A third trend was the greater understanding and acceptance of optimisation, simulation and other decision models from the discipline of Management Science/Operations Research (MS/OR) and a growing recognition of the power of integrating such models in information-system applications. The *decision support phase* of the information-system field could be traced to the convergence of the above developments. In this chapter we will be primarily concerned with models and concepts of decisions to which we now turn. We also discuss the implications of these concepts for the design of systems to support decision making.

2.2 Decision-making Perspectives

Decision making can be studied from various perspectives. The economist is concerned with individual and social choices relating to production and consumption against the backdrop of limited resources through the mechanisms of prices and markets. The psychologist is concerned with the limits of human cognitive capacity and how they influence decision making especially when the problem complexity is high. The management scientist attempts to mathematically model the decision and to develop rules for optimal or near-optimal solution and to develop computational algorithms for implementing the solution. The approach of the economist and the management scientist can generally be characterised as normative in that they address the question of how people *ought* to make decisions in various types of situations if they are to be regarded as rational. The psychologist and the organisation theorist take a more descriptive view, according to which the objective is to investigate and describe how people *actually make* decisions in a variety of situations. Normative-decision theory is more precise and formal by virtue of the abstract and idealised representations of the decisions it employs. In contrast, descriptive-decision theory deals with real-life situations in all their complexity. It strives for realism at the expense of precision and logical elegance. It also addresses itself to the problem of understanding the organisational context within which much of the decision making takes place. We will present a range of concepts and frameworks that pertain to these models of decision making in this chapter.

2.3 The Process of Decision Making

Herbert Simon and his colleagues, from what has come to be known as the Carnegie School, have developed a simple yet powerful model of the process of decision making. In its original form it comprised three distinct yet interrelated phases, namely, *intelligence, design* and *choice* (Simon, 1977). Subsequently, a fourth phase – *review and implementation* – was added to this model.

The intelligence phase primarily involves scanning the environment and searching for information that would suggest the existence of a problem (or opportunity) and the need for a decision. There is some evidence from comprehensive studies of what managers and executives actually do to indicate that much of their time is spent in gathering, processing and transmitting information using a range of sources and media (Mintzberg, 1973). This activity is generally more about open-ended scanning rather than highly focused searching for specific information, though at certain times the intelligence phase can become more directed. The goal of this phase is to alert the individual to potential problems that need to be addressed and/or opportunities to be followed up.

For a good understanding of different decision-making phases, it is useful to study a specific hypothetical example of a decision problem in an organisation. Laura Alvarado is the marketing manager of a large cosmetics company in the mid-1990s. During the *intelligence phase* she learned, from conversations with counterparts in other consumer-goods firms and from scanning the business media, of the growing impact of electronic marketing. While the cosmetics industry had not embraced this channel for doing business in a big way, there were clear indications that increasing proportions of both business-to-consumer and business-to-business sales will be carried out through the Worldwide Web (WWW) on the Internet. Some reliable forecasts pointed to a trillion US dollar overall sales turnover through the Internet by 2002. She followed this up through discussions with knowledgeable people, consultants and her own colleagues. She also pored through trade publications and checked with industry sources to learn more about what the competitors have been doing in the electronic arena. Additionally, she looked up some of the websites of major competitors to assess for herself the extent to which her competitors have progressed in terms of opening up web-based advertising and sales outlets and the strategies they employ. She also started to think about the effect of her organisation's potential foray into electronic marketing on sales through existing channels.

Once the contours of a problem have been recognised, *the design phase* involves a set of activities related to identifying, formulating and analysing a set of viable alternatives that can lead to a resolution of the problem. A large number of candidate alternatives may initially be explored and subsequently reduced to a smaller and manageable subset. These are subjected to rigorous analysis in terms of the likely consequences of each. Depending on the decision-making styles and analytical capabilities available, this analysis can have both quantitative and qualitative dimensions. The former may involve the development of models for forecasting, financial and market-share analyses, etc. The qualitative overview is usually performed by pooling the *experiential and tacit knowledge* possessed by key organisational participants regarding each of the alternatives and their likely consequences. Experiential knowledge refers to that gained by experience which is typically rooted in the organisational context and which can be reasonably articulated. Tacit knowledge, on the other hand, is that which is relatively more broad based and acquired over a longer period of time and is difficult to explicitly articulate. Clearly the two interact to produce an outcome.

In response to the problem faced by Laura Alvarado, some of the alternatives that emerged as the decision process unfolded were:

1. comprehensive electronic-marketing option by establishing a major web presence through which customers can order any of the company's products. Payments can be made using credit cards through a secure server and the goods can be directly shipped to customers in any part of the world;
2. a limited electronic-marketing initiative in which the company establishes a website primarily for advertising and dissemination of product-related information. This site will also be used to gather information about customers which will be passed on to relevant dealer outlets. The relatively stronger ones will be encouraged and provided the technical and organisational assistance for launching their own Internet marketing operations; and
3. the default option of continuing to scan the market while waiting for firmer trends to materialise.

In the *choice phase*, the decision maker chooses one of the alternatives from the set generated and analysed in the design phase. This is typically based on a number of criteria, some of which are crisp and precise while others are somewhat intangible and ambiguous. There is also the question of the degree of uncertainty and risk attached to each of the alternatives. The trade-offs among the alternatives is an important aspect of the choice phase. To the extent that the design phase is carried out comprehensively, the complexity of the choice phase is reduced.

Choosing one of the three options listed above was fraught with difficulty for Laura Alvarado, given the economic, technological and market-related uncertainties. While it is true that the number of Internet users and the value of business transacted electronically have been growing exponentially, no good data on the electronic-shopping habits of cosmetics customers were available. The impact of opting for the Internet channel on sales through existing channels needed to be estimated. This will be closely related to the pricing decisions for Internet trading. Many cosmetics customers like to try out the products in department stores and there were doubts as to whether they will be enamoured of Internet stores, except perhaps for routine purchases. The comparative costs of providing services to the customers through the Internet over other channels needed to be estimated and weighed against the potential benefits of reaching out to new customers and the ability to gather information about individual customers using the Internet channel. There were also uncertainties regarding the technical capabilities of the company's Information Technology (IT) Group for getting the complex electronic-commerce application developed, tested and implemented in reasonable time, not to mention the myriad security risks associated with Internet trading in general. The second and third alternatives represent a more cautious approach. The viability of the second is largely dependent on the enthusiasm of the dealers and retail outlets. There is also the opportunity cost of not engaging the electronic channel early and starting to climb the learning curve and the risk of being surprised by a new or existing competitor who reaps the rewards that accrue to the prime mover under both second and third alternatives. The absence of a single and clearcut decision criterion such as net profit over a 5-year horizon or total costs or estimated market share added to the difficulty in reaching the 'right' decision.

The fourth and final phase is that of *review and implementation*. This again is a complex set of decisions made over a period of time during which the chosen solution is actually accepted by a variety of stakeholders and carried out over time. The tasks are assigned to different individuals and groups and the progress against each is reviewed periodically.

Several comments about the above process model are in order. First, the term 'decision making' is interpreted very broadly as to become almost synonymous with managing. Each phase involves a number of smaller decisions and activities. Some authors associate the term 'decision making' with only the moment of choice but that is just the tip of the iceberg. The phases closely mirror the classic problem-solving stages proposed by the pragmatic American philosopher John Dewey:

> *What is the problem?*
> *What are the alternatives?*
> *Which alternative is the best?*   (Dewey, 1910 cited in Simon, 1977).

Second, there is no clear temporal sequence by which design follows intelligence and choice follows design. For complex decisions, each phase gives rise to new sub-problems which may call for a separate intelligence–design–choice cycle. The phases may also overlap considerably with the choice phase calling for more design activities and so on. The model is best thought of as a stylised representation but we would expect the three major phases to be clearly discernible as complex decision processes unfold (Simon, 1977, p. 43).

Third, a group of individuals is likely to be involved in decision making rather than a single eminently rational decision maker. Furthermore, decision making will be played out against the context of the organisation and its norms, structures and procedures. Alternative models of the process of such decision making have been proposed. The organisational-procedures perspective attempts to understand decisions as the resultant of multiple standard operating procedures invoked by various organisational subunits. This view emphasises the structure of the organisation in terms of the roles of the participants, rules and procedures and channels of communication (Allison, 1971; Cyert and March, 1963). The political perspective focuses on the bargaining process between various organisational groups and subunits. Decisions are arrived at incrementally as compromises among competing interest groups and shifting coalitions (Pettigrew, 1976).

Finally, organisations are faced with decisions which are highly varied in terms of their complexity, degree of structure, level at which they are dealt with and the number of people involved. In the next section we deal with some of the distinctions. A good understanding of these is important for enabling us to make judicious choices about the right kind of decisions for which to build support artefacts and systems and how to go about building them.

2.4 Structure and Typology of Decisions

The degree of 'programmability' or structuredness is a conceptually useful dimension for understanding and classifying decisions. In his book *The New Science of Management Decision*, Simon (1977) argued that decisions could be placed along a spectrum from completely programmed to completely unprogrammed. The following quotations from the book illuminates the distinction cogently:

> *Decisions are unprogrammed to the extent that they are repetitive and routine, to the extent that a definite procedure has been worked out for handling them so that they don't have to treated de novo each time they occur.*

> *Decisions are unprogrammed to the extent that they are novel, unstructured and unusually consequential. There is no cut-and-dried method for handling the problem because it has not arisen before, or because its precise nature and structure are elusive or complex, or because it is so important that it deserves custom-tailored treatment.*   (Simon, 1977, p. 47)

Programmed or structured decisions are sufficiently repetitive as to enable the development of program or procedure that can be routinely invoked. Examples include reordering low and medium-value inventory items and allocating performance bonuses to sales personnel. They are characterised by crisp and certain decision criteria, a limited number of well-defined alternatives whose consequences can be worked out without much difficulty. Non-programmed or unstructured decisions involve problems for which a precise procedure cannot or has not been worked out and the organisation has to fall back on its capacity for adaptive problem-oriented action. The absence of a single well-understood-decision criterion and the difficulty in identifying and developing a compact and finite set of alternatives and the high levels of uncertainty concerning the consequences of the known alternatives at most of the decision stages, are all expressions of this unstructuredness. The decision situation dealt with by Laura Alvarado as to whether or not to launch electronic marketing referred to earlier or the decision of a company to establish operations in a country where it has not operated before are examples of relatively unstructured decisions. It is possible that such problems are decomposable into phases and subproblems, some of which are well structured. Most real-world problems fall somewhere towards the unstructured end of this spectrum and are depicted in Figure 2.1.

Another classification scheme, based on the levels of managerial activity, has been provided by Anthony (1965). Based on the view that organisations are essentially hierarchical in their form, he identified three levels, namely, *strategic planning,*

Programmed or well-structured decisions	Non-programmed or unstructured decisions
– Routine and repetitive – A program or clear procedure can be invoked for making the decision – Decision criteria are crisp and well defined – The number of alternatives are few and the consequences of each are not difficult to evaluate	– Novel and infrequent – No known or tested procedure exists for making the decision – Decision criteria are imprecise and poorly understood – Alternatives are numerous, overlapping and the consequences of each are hard to enumerate and assess

Figure 2.1. The decision spectrum based on the degree of programmability (adapted from Simon, 1977).

management control and *operational control*. Strategic planning is the purview of senior managers and it deals with setting the long-term goals of the organisation and policies for the acquisition, deployment and monitoring of diverse organisational resources to achieve these goals. There is a nexus of typically unstructured decisions to be made at this level. Management-control decisions involve the allocation of resources and ensuring effective utilisation of resources within the framework of the policies and constraints imposed by strategic planning. Operational control refers to decisions at the base of the organisational pyramid concerned with ensuring that concrete projects and tasks are carried out effectively and efficiently. The decisions at this level are likely to be relatively well structured and less ambiguous though some of them can still be computationally quite complex.

Gorry and Scott Morton have suggested that the characteristics of information that will be more appropriate for many the strategic decisions, with their limited degree of structure, will be vastly different from those needed for making operational decisions. The former will require predictions about the future more than accurate historical information. Generally speaking, the information needed for strategic decisions will tend to be aggregate information obtained from external sources. The scope and variety of the information demanded would be wide and open ended. Laura Alvarado's decision was facilitated more by information obtained from external sources, such as customers, advertising agencies, Internet channel consultants and other organisations with previous experience in this form of marketing, than by information gathered from internal sources. The scope of the necessary information tended to be broad based and covered a wide range of relevant issues and topics. She was to use significant amount of forecast-type information at a high level of aggregation and coarse granularity than she would for deciding on sales quotas for salespersons in different regions.

The operational decisions, in sharp contrast, need very different kinds of information. Given their specific task orientation, the right information for these decisions will be well defined and narrow in scope, based largely on accurate historical data, internally sourced and very detailed. It is also likely that the frequency of use of this information will be high. Management-control decisions tend to fall between the two extremes with respect to the characteristics of information that will be needed (Gorry and Scott Morton, 1971).

An alternative classification of decisions, based on the availability of models to solve underlying problems, has been proposed by Ackoff (1967). It consists of three types:

1.   Decisions for which adequate models are available or can be constructed from which optimal or near-optimal solutions can be developed. The challenge in these problems

is to effectively integrate the decision into the information systems. This model will also identify what information is needed for decision making.

2. Decisions for which adequate models could be constructed but the problem complexity in computational terms is such that optimal solutions cannot be found. Here, some heuristic search or data-driven procedures may need to be developed to identify and evaluate the alternatives.

3. Decisions for which adequate models cannot be constructed. In these situations, comprehensive analysis of the processes employed by decision makers to address the problem need to carried out so that one can begin to unravel the implicit problem structure and to identify information requirements. Only certain parts of the problem may lend themselves to systemic solutions but other parts may call for managerial intuition and judgment.

Another useful distinction that has implications for building DSSs has been proposed by Donovan and Madnick (1977). In their view, organisational decisions could be *institutional* or ad hoc. Decisions are institutional to the extent that the underlying problems are recurrent and the same or closely related decisions have to be made periodically. The decision contexts are somewhat stable, making it worthwhile to design support systems which can be refined and improved over time. There is the possibility of continuous learning by decision makers leading to consistent decision outcomes. Even for highly complex yet recurrent decisions, the decision makers are able to develop effective heuristics and decision processes that can be tapped into by systems designers. Examples of institutional decisions include ongoing determination of the money to be spent on various forms of advertising and in-store promotion for each product by a mature consumer-product marketing company or investment-portfolio management decisions by an insurance company.

Ad hoc decisions, on the other hand, relate to problem situations that are non-recurrent and hence not easily anticipated and analysed. Because they tend to be one-off or arise very rarely, the decision-making process has to rely greatly on managerial judgment and adaptive problem solving. Laura Alvarado's problem has all the hallmarks of a highly unstructured ad hoc decision with major short- and long-term consequences. Supporting this class of decisions from a system-design perspective presents special challenges since parts of the overall problem that can be modelled need to be isolated, modelled and implemented as systems. This needs to be done in a dynamic fashion by adapting and integrating known tools and by reusing elements of previous solutions.

2.5 Rational Decision-making Models and the Limits of Human Cognitive Capacity

The rational model of decision making has a long pedigree in fields like economics and management science/operations research. It is essentially normative and prescriptive in that it starts out with an abstract representation of the real-world problem and outlines a procedure for generating an optimal solution to the represented problem. The procedure involves the identification of all discrete and mutually exclusive alternatives and the criteria or utilities which reflect the preference structure of the decision maker. It also assumes that a quantified value representing the score for each alternative against each criterion can be obtained. If multiple criteria are present, it is assumed that the relative importance or weights attached to each criterion are known. Given all these, a number of techniques have been developed for choosing or rank ordering the alternatives so as to maximise utility (maximise profit, minimise waste, etc.). Decision analysis, cost-benefit analysis, break-even analysis, economic-order-quantity (EOQ) analysis and mathematical programming are examples of such techniques and they have been successfully applied for a wide range of problems. Most good management-science textbooks provide detailed and step-by-step methods for rational problem solving. See Daellenbach (1994) for a very comprehensive methodological discussion.

Consider the following decision problem faced by Nancy Clare, the Promotions Manager of a software firm, who is trying to decide on the venue for the upcoming European Windows Users' Conference (adapted from Daellenbach, 1994). This meeting is always preceded by a number of workshops sponsored by various special interest groups. Geneva was chosen as the conference city. Nancy identified four potential venues – A (a first-class airport hotel), B (a luxury city-centre hotel), C (a university-conference venue) and D (a newly renovated chateau in a nearby village) – for a shortlist and visited each of them and noted the important aspects of each. She then proceeded to come up with a list of objectives considered important for evaluating each alternative venue. Based on consultations with all the members of the conference organising committee she organised a pre-conference workshop to elicit and prioritise the criteria. The following list was produced:

1. overall cost of the facility
2. ease of transport access
3. quality of conference rooms and other conference facilities
4. quality of accommodation
5. catering service for conference meals
6. staff experience and helpfulness
7. availability of and easy access to informal social meeting places and restaurants
8. overall environment of the venue.

It was not very difficult for Nancy to rearrange the criteria in the following hierarchical fashion since the objectives fall into three distinct groups as follows:

- **Location:** Access
             Overall environment
- **Facilities:** Accommodation
             Catering
             Conference rooms
             Staff experience
             Social meeting places
- **Cost**

Location, facilities and cost are known as first-level criteria and the others are second-level criteria.

The next step is to assess the relative importance of each criterion by assigning weights to each. One convenient way of doing this is to elicit, from relevant stakeholders, values between 0 and 1 so that they add up to 1 for first-level criteria, and similarly the weights of second-level criteria associated with each first-level criterion, so as to add up to 1 and so on. The values obtained by Nancy, by averaging the figures provided by the workshop participants, can be seen in the second and third columns of Figure 2.2. The weights represent the importance the decision makers attach to each criterion and determining this can be difficult. As we shall see later in this chapter, the decision makers may be prone to a number of biases in assigning the weights which they may not be fully aware of.

Criteria	Weights		Scores for venue			
	Level 1	Level 2	A	B	C	D
Location:	0.35					
Environment		0.50	0	25	40	100
Acess		0.50	100	80	35	0
Facilities:	0.45					
Staff experience		0.10	100	80	40	0
Conference rooms		0.30	75	100	50	0
Social meeting		0.15	25	100	0	75
Accommodation		0.20	80	100	0	90
Catering		0.25	60	70	0	100
Cost	0.20		5	0	100	60
Evaluation						
	Location		50.0	52.5	37.5	50.0
	Facilities		67.5	90.5	19.0	54.3
	Cost		5.0	0.0	100.0	60.0
	Overall Score		48.8	59.1	39.9	53.9

Figure 2.2. Evaluation of conference venues (from Daellenbach, 1994, p. 512).

The scores awarded by the committee to each of the venues against each criterion on a 1–100 scale are shown in columns 4–7 of Figure 2.2. At this point the weighted score for each alternative against each first-level criterion and the overall score can be computed to produce a rank ordering of the four venues.

Another illustration of rational decision making from economics involves an entrepreneurial decision maker faced with calculating the number of widgets to manufacture in order to maximise profit. The cost curve relating cost to the number of widgets produced and the revenue curve relating sales to the number of widgets sold are known. For this highly simplified problem situation, the challenge for the entrepreneur is to decide on the number of widgets Q to be manufactured for each time period so as to maximise the difference between total revenues and total costs. Formulated in this form, this is a simple mathematical problem which can be solved for the optimal value of Q.

The decision system presented in both the above illustrations can be described as *substantively* rational. Given an abstract representation of the problem and one or more very specific criteria, this can provide a normative approach to finding the right course of action. However, it tells us very little about how the concerned actors actually go about framing the problem and making the decisions. The lack of realism and descriptive validity of the model has been the focus of some of the most interesting writings of Simon who argued that such models do not possess the *procedural* rationality needed when the decision-making process has to be adapted to the contingencies of real-world complexities (Simon, 1969). From the point of view of descriptive validity of the models, Simon argued that humans cannot possess the information-processing capabilities needed to process all the information implied by the rational model. The entrepreneur in the previous example needs to consider a whole host of additional issues, such as quality of widget, uncertainty with respect to demand, changes over time in costs and myriad other concrete details that impact on the decision about the quantity of widgets to produce. Not every one of these is precisely quantifiable to the degree the rational model would suggest. He termed this limit on human cognitive capacity, which causes the gap between substantive and procedural rationality, as *bounded rationality*. Based on behaviourally grounded studies of how people actually went about making complex decisions, he concluded that these limits on human information processing and computational capacity led to people making *satisficing* decisions when confronted by most real-world problems. In sharp contrast to optimising, satisficing implies that people use a variety of simplifying mechanisms and heuristics to arrive at a solution that they are comfortable with, though not necessarily optimal. To quote Simon (1969):

> *In the real world we usually do not have a choice between satisfactory and optimal solution, for we rarely have a method of finding the optimum.*

> *We cannot, within practicable computational limits, generate all the admissible alternatives and compare their relative merits. Nor can we recognise the best alternative, even if we are fortunate enough to generate it early, until we have seen all of them. We satisfice by looking for alternatives in such a way that we can generally find an acceptable one after only moderate search*   (Simon, 1969, p. 64).

Researchers, working in the field of cognitive science on the problem of how human minds function in making decisions, have confirmed the extensive use of heuristics which help us cope with complexity. These rules of thumb serve as important props to decision making and can be incorporated into computer aids to support decision making. However, some of them introduce systematic biases into the decision processes and outcomes. We will briefly discuss some of the more systematic heuristics and biases, first uncovered by Tversky and Kahneman (1974, 1986).

- *Availability Heuristic.* People rely to an extreme degree on occurrences fresh in their memory when making judgments on probability or the likely causes of an event. A member of the organising committee, ranking the four venue alternatives to choose the conference hotel, is likely to be unduly influenced in his ratings by a highly positive or negative experience in one of those hotels in the recent past.
- *Representative Heuristic.* Decision makers tend to assess the likelihood of an event by the extent to which the occurrence of the event is similar to stereotypes of similar occurrences. In hiring programmers, good or poor performance by a few employees from a particular ethnic group can lead to a stereotyped perception of the programming ability of members of that group in general. A variant of this heuristic is insensitivity to sample size. For instance, Laura Alvarado's decision on the Internet channel could be influenced by the negative reactions to buying through the Internet that she picked up in recent conversations with some of customers and dealers, even though they were unlikely to be a representative sample.
- *Anchoring and Adjustment.* In making decisions, people seem to give undue weight to historical data or first information or estimates they receive. These serve as anchors against which judgments are calibrated and adjusted. To the extent that the anchors are off base, significant errors can creep into decisions.
- *Framing Bias.* The original form in which a problem gets framed tends to dictate the subsequent flow of the decision-making process. The Internet channel decision could be

framed purely as a marketing problem about maintaining and improving market share, as Laura Alvarado seems to have done, or as an organisational strategic issue for aligning technical, marketing and organisational capabilities to the changing global business environment. The latter framing could result in greater involvement by the Managing Director or Chief Executive Officer (CEO) of the company and much more resources being committed to reaching the right decision.

2.6 Implications for Application Design

We use the term 'model' to usually refer to a convenient abstraction of reality. Hence, modelling as a system-design principle is a fundamental approach to dealing with problem-solving complexities by working through appropriate abstractions. From a design perspective then, models are built and used for a variety of purposes. Rouse and Morris (1986) identify three recurring themes in the literature about the purpose of models: to describe the purpose and form of a system, to explain the functioning and state of a system and finally to predict the future state of a system. This integrated view of the purposes of mental models is illustrated in Figure 2.3 and is applicable to models in general.

The *structure* of the model describes the form of the system and the *behaviour* of the model explains its functioning. The model structure instantiated with data describes a particular state of the system. Varying the parameters that control the behaviour of the model allows the prediction of possible future states of the system.

In the context of design, a model can be viewed as a device for predicting the output from a real system, under various conditions specified by the input data, without actually using the real system to make this prediction. This is illustrated in Figure 2.4 (Mitchell, 1993).

As shown in Figure 2.3, it is possible to transform data about the system to information that could be used for predicting the behaviour of the system through two routes. Route A uses the data on the real system, but this could be costly. Route B uses the model and provides an alternative medium to conduct experiments and *what-if* analysis with less risk. It allows the decision maker to understand the problem better and analyse systematically the complexities of the problem. Route B involves the following steps: (1) conversion of real-world data into model data that is suited to the way the model is represented or

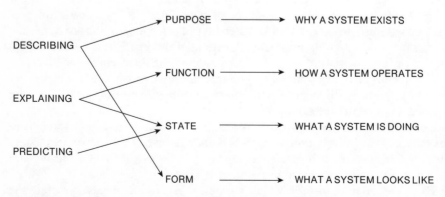

Figure 2.3. Purposes of mental models (from Rouse and Morris, 1986).

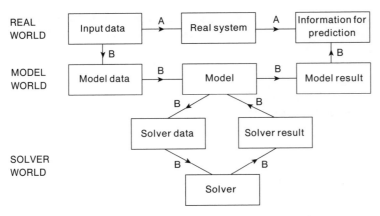

Figure 2.4. Model as a device (adapted from Mitchell, 1993).

implemented; (2) storage of the data as a model instance; (3) there may be a further conversion of model data into data that the algorithm/solver can use; (4) solution of model instance by a solver; (5) there may be a conversion of solver results into model results; (6) finally there will be conversion of model results into information that could be used for prediction.

When we consider an environment where we can carry out the kind of modelling depicted above, many design-process issues arise. A proper design approach should cover all aspects of the modelling life cycle in order to provide adequate support of the use of such an environment. Geoffrion (1989) refers to this process as providing cradle-to-grave support for modelling. The specific phases that are important to consider as part of such a process can be outlined as follows:

- formulation of the model – support the modeller in the creation of the model;
- integration of the model with data/instantiation of the model – support the modeller in the instantiation of the model;
- integration of the model with appropriate solvers – allow the modeller to link to a variety of solver technologies;
- use/execution of the model – allow the modeller to solve the problem using a particular instance of the model;
- analysing, reporting and explaining the results of the model;
- perform *what-if* analysis on the model by changing the assumptions about the task at hand;
- reformulation of the model if necessary.

These phases do not necessarily occur in sequence and several phases would be revisited over the modelling life cycle. It is important to keep these process aspects in mind as we work our way through several examples of design in the subsequent chapters of this book.

2.7 Summary

Our primary focus in this chapter is on the structure of decisions and the process of decision making in organisations. We discuss the terminology and concepts related to the modern view of organisations as information processing and decision-making entities.

Process models of the decision-making phases and various typologies of decisions are reviewed. We have contrasted the textbook rational decision-making model with the more realistic descriptive models. In the process the chapter explores the key differences between an optimisation approach as opposed to a heuristic problem-solving framework. Some of the systematic biases that get introduced into heuristic decision processes are outlined. Finally, we have linked many of these concepts to design implications. This is important for us to understand salient design principles that will allow us to build the class of applications which is the focus of this book.

References

Ackoff, R. L. (1967) Management misinformation systems, *Management Science*, **14**(4), B147–B156.

Allison, G. T. (1971) *Essence of Decision: Examining the Cuban Missile Crisis*, Boston: Little, Brown.

Anthony, R. N. (1965) *Planning and Control Systems: A Framework for Analysis*, Cambridge, MA: Harvard University Graduate School of Business Administration.

Cyert, R. M. and March, J. G. (1963) *A Behavioral Theory of the Firm*, Englewood Cliffs, NJ: Prentice-Hall.

Daellenbach, H. G. (1994) *Systems and Decision Making*, Chichester: Wiley.

Dewey, J. (1910) *How We Think*, New York: D. C. Heath.

Donovan, J. J. and Madnick, S. E. (1977) Institutional and ad hoc decision support systems and their effective use, *Database*, **8**(3), 79–88.

Geoffrion, A. M. (1989) Computer-based modelling environments, *European Journal of Operational Research*, **41**, 33–45.

Gorry, G. A. and Scott Morton, M. S. (1971) A framework for management information systems, *Sloan Management Review*, **13**(1), 55–70.

Mintzberg, H. (1973) *The Nature of Managerial Work*, Englewood Cliffs, NJ: Prentice-Hall.

Mitchell, G. (1993) *The Practice of Operational Research*, John Wiley and Sons, New York.

Pettigrew, A. (1976) *The Politics of Organisational Decision Making*, London: Tavistock.

Rouse, W. B. and Morris, N. M. (1986) On looking into the black box: Prospects and limits in the search for mental models, *Psychological Bulletin*, **100**(3), 349–363.

Simon, H. A. (1957) A behavioral model of rational choice. In H. A. Simon (ed.), *Models of Man*, New York: Wiley, pp. 241–260.

Simon, H. A. (1969) *The Sciences of the Artificial*, Cambridge, MA: MIT Press.

Simon, H. A. (1977) *The New Science of Management Decision* (revised edition), Englewood Cliffs, NJ: Prentice-Hall.

Tversky, A. and Kahneman, D. (1974) Judgement under uncertainty: Heuristics and biases, *Science*, **185**, 1,124–1,131.

Tversky, A. and Kahneman, D. (1986) Rational choice and the framing of decisions, *Journal of Business*, **4**(2), S251–258.

DISCUSSION QUESTIONS

1. Identify a decision-making situation that you have recently confronted and the steps that you took in resolving it.
2. Describe in your own words how the four phases of decision making proposed by Herbert Simon apply to the decision-making situation described in #1.
3. Identify decisions that will fall into each of the major categories offered by the following frameworks discussed in this chapter:
   - structured – unstructured tasks;
   - strategic planning, management control, operational control;

- Gorry and Scott Morton's framework that juxtaposes task structure and managerial level;
- Ackoff's model availability;
- Institutional versus ad hoc decision making.

4. Describe a situation where using a model would be appropriate as opposed to testing hypotheses on the 'real world'.

5. What are some technical challenges that you can think of for the design of a system that supports 'cradle-to-grave' modelling.

3
The Technology to Support Decision Making

3.1 Architectural Framework for Discourse

Decision support applications have a set of technological requirements that need to be met for design purposes. In order to understand what is commonly available by way of capabilities, we need a framework for discourse about these applications and their specific requirements. In this chapter, we provide an overview of some important technology platforms that are commonly available and can be utilised to build the class of systems that we have talked about thus far. We do this by taking the perspective of a typical application of interest and then addressing the IT support requirements at the conceptual and the specific implementation levels. The questions of interest in this chapter are: (a) given the class of decision-making problems that we wish to support with the use of IT, what technology-based capabilities are essential to realise design products and (b) what are some representative platforms that are able to deliver these capabilities. Figure 3.1 captures the framework for our discussion in this chapter.

Taking a task-oriented perspective, a problem instance occurs in a particular organisational context. For example, an organisational context might be in the area of customer support in a high-technology firm. Typical applications might include such things as help-desk management, special-order configuration, product servicing, etc. Task instances are specific issues that need resolution within this general organisational context in which the problems occur. An example of a problem that needs to be addressed might be an

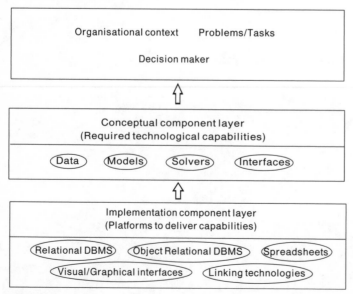

Figure 3.1. Architectural framework.

investigation of how to improve customer satisfaction with special orders. Addressing such a problem by a decision maker would typically involve exploring the details of the context that is relevant to the task at hand. When we talk about supporting such a task with information technology, there are some broad categories of support that are meaningful. We refer to these categories collectively as the 'conceptual component layer'. This layer specifies, in general terms, what categories of technologies are most useful in responding to the support requirements in a typical application. Analysing the framework further, categories in the conceptual component layer must translate to specific design capabilities that will enable us to build systems. In other words, our motivation to talk about the *implementation of systems* must be backed up by pointers to specific tools of design. By describing representative tools that are well known and exist in the marketplace, we can talk in a concrete manner about implementation by linking categories in the conceptual component layer with implementation-level components. This last layer is referred to in Figure 3.1 as the 'implementation component layer'. It is important to emphasise here that not all problems require an explicit interaction with *all* the conceptual and implementation layer components with equal vigour. The particular nature of the problem will dictate the relativities with which the various components are brought to bear on a solution method. A model-intensive application will clearly rely more heavily on those components that address that particular capability. Conversely, a data-intensive problem will rely on data-oriented components. The examples of various organisational contexts and associated problems throughout this book illustrate the reliance on different components of this architecture in a manner that depends on the context.

3.1.1 The Conceptual Component Layer

The framework for discussion revolves around the support that is required to enhance the quality of decision making. Essentially this translates to supporting a decision maker engaged in problem-solving activities in a particular application domain. As stated in our previous examples, it is useful to think about such support as consisting essentially of the following capabilities:

- *Data – handling large volumes of data:* This facilitates the need to rely on data and their relationships to formulate data-oriented questions, the answers to which can be efficiently retrieved.
- *Models – ability to describe and maintain (possibly non-trivial) models that define rules for manipulating the data:* This facilitates the expression of data-manipulation rules that describe ways through which useful results can be produced by utilising the contents of databases. Such rules may be defined and stored on an ongoing basis as part of a library or alternatively defined on an as-needed basis.
- *Solvers – having a mechanism to translate model specifications to implementable system components:* This facilitates the implementation of manipulation rules for the data. We want to separate the specification of the rules from their implementation so that we have the flexibility to choose how manipulation rules are implemented.
- *Interfaces – providing a powerful vehicle for user interaction with system components:* This enhances the usability of design products, which is particularly important if we are to encourage a user community with diverse skill sets to engage in leveraging the technology for decision making.

3.1.2 The Implementation Component Layer

At the implementation level, there are powerful yet commonly available platforms that are capable of delivering the requirements from the conceptual component layer. We briefly describe what these are and then provide examples of the usage of each of these components.

- *Relational Database Management Systems:* These systems primarily support the data-management requirements of applications. The technology has been around for over 25 years and several commercially available systems are widely used. These systems present a tabular view of data to the user and retrieval is denoted by the specification of filtering rules (selection criteria) by the user. They are capable of handling large volumes of data efficiently and the interfaces to provide access to the data have developed and matured over the years. Some of these systems provide links to programming languages and this capability may be used to implement models and solvers.
- *Object Relational Database Management Systems:* This is a relatively new class of systems that builds on the benefits of relational technology. The object orientation of these system allows the capture of complex data and their relationships. Furthermore, some of these systems are well integrated to allow the specification of data-manipulation rules. Such rules can be expressed using procedural programming languages and declarative database-access languages. These capabilities are well suited for model and solver specification.
- *Spreadsheets:* This is a class of systems that is fundamental to personal computing. It has wide user acceptance and utilises a familiar rows-and-columns paradigm for representing data. The power of these systems lies in their ability to incorporate manipulation rules for data and to instantly view the results of such manipulation expressions. Additionally, they are ideal environments to examine alternative task scenarios and conduct sensitivity analyses of particular problems. They provide a useful capability to support the implementation of models and solvers.
- *Visual Interfaces:* The manner in which the user interacts with a system can largely determine how useful the application really is. With decision support applications, it is critical that we try and incorporate visually oriented access mechanisms to encourage a wider set of users to utilise the technology. Some platforms such as spreadsheet environments have many built-in features that are visually oriented. Typically these include graphing of data, in different forms. Database systems have made a concerted effort over the years to provide visual ways of interacting with application data, in addition to more traditional access mechanisms. Usually this has meant the use of icons to facilitate the need for visually based interaction with the system. If we are to make applications useful, this visual approach must be explored fully in the context of design. We refer to this idea as the 'visual imperative'.
- *Linking Technologies:* Our approach to designing applications involves the ability to bring different enabling technologies together in a design context. For example, it is important to have the capability of developing different parts of a single application using different development platforms but use linking mechanisms between the platforms to deliver the final design product. This enables us to elegantly address the conceptual components of design under a single umbrella by considering their development using different design tools.

We now turn to an elaboration of each of the enabling platforms that we have discussed under the implementation component layer. We do this by developing illustrative examples using current platforms that are easily available from commercial vendors.

3.2 Relational Databases

Relational database management grew out of a concept and some implementation ideas initially proposed about three decades ago by E. F. Codd (Codd, 1970). Some basic issues that were addressed by the relational approach at that time were:

- data can be a valuable organisational resource;
- data must be shareable across multiple users;
- data must be accessible conveniently by a large user community;
- data access may be routine and pre-planned or non-routine and ad hoc.

These issues translated to a platform design prescription that data-management systems must simultaneously be intuitively accessible by a wide user community while providing a facility to maintain a large store of persistent of data in an efficient manner. It is the combination of this dual concern that made the concept appealing. Up until this ground-breaking proposal was first made, while there existed a recognition that managing data was of vital importance to organisations, the implementation platforms were non-intuitive and complex to use. The idea of relational systems opened up the possibility that these platforms could cater for the data-management aspirations of a whole new class of users.

In spite of the obvious appeal of the relational approach, the accessibility that it promised did not extend to hardware platforms that were available in the 1970s. It was not until the arrival of the personal computer that relational systems gained wide user acceptance. Since the introduction of the personal computer, rapid advances in the capabilities of personal workstations and networking technologies have combined forces with a number of commercial developers to make relational systems the platform of choice for data management.

3.2.1 Basic Structures

The most basic structure in which to store and manage data in a relational platform is the *relation*. In an operational sense, a relation is viewed by the user as a two-dimensional table. The columns in the table stand for the properties or descriptors of data classes of interest in an application. The rows in the table contain the data values that correspond to the descriptors. Each row of data is thus made up of multiple data values, all of which collectively correspond to a single instance of the class that is represented in the table. The intuitive appeal of such a perspective on data is obvious.

Consider an application where we are interested in storing and managing data about active projects in an organisation. PROJECT is a *class* of data that is important in our application. Since there may be several projects about which data needs to be managed, each project is an *instance* of this class. Having determined that the class PROJECT should be built into our design, we have to consider the most useful manner in which the data aspects of this class can be described. In other words, what are the salient properties or attributes of each project that would be important enough to capture in the application? The following may make up such a set in a typical situation:[1]

Figure 3.2 presents a list of useful attributes that describe each project. This is important input to the design process. Each attribute is identified by (1) a label shown in the first column of the table, (2) the meaning of the attribute shown in the second

---

[1] Note that the construction of an appropriate list of class attributes will usually come from somebody who has a good understanding of the application domain and is therefore in a position to comment on the importance of the attributes selected for inclusion in the design.

Attribute 1 label	Description	Example values
PROJECT-ID	A unique identifier of a project	A-2002, B-1988, C-1031, etc.
PROJECT-TYPE	The type of project based on its characteristics	STRATEGIC, OPERATIONAL, TACTICAL, etc.
BUDGET	The allocated budget for a project	$300,000, etc.
DOMESTIC-MARKET	The type of consumer market that the project will impact: domestic or international?	TRUE (if domestic), FALSE (if international) (*Note: only two market types are defined*)
START-DATE	Date on which the project commenced	1 January 1997, etc.
MANAGER	The name of the person who is designated as the project manager	ABLE, BAKER, CHARLES, etc.

Figure 3.2. Relational database structure.

column of the table (the semantics that underlie the attribute – what does it mean?) and (3) examples of values that the data can assume (once we start capturing it from the organisation) shown in the third column of the table. It is also important to point out that each attribute is of a particular data type: numeric, date, character, etc. Relational database systems typically offer a limited set of such types into which application data must be mapped. Each of the data types is associated with a defined collection of allowable operations on data belonging to that type. For example, arithmetic computations can be performed on numeric data. In essence then, what we have described here is a template or structure for the data as far as projects are concerned. Clearly several data classes may be relevant in an application. Each one must be defined in the manner shown above and included as part of the application. Let us first explore the case of the PROJECT table (Figure 3.3).

If we now populate Figure 3.2 with some data, it might begin to look like Figure 3.3. Figures 3.2 and 3.3 in combination give us an idea about the structure and contents of what we have designed to capture data about projects. We have a list of six attributes that describe projects – the structure of the PROJECT class. In Figure 3.3 we have captured data about 12 projects in a manner that corresponds to the previously defined structure. This is shown as 12 rows of data in the table, each one consisting of a collection of data values that together are descriptive of a single project. The structure itself is seen as something that is relatively stable and persists as part of the application as long as we are interested (as users) in maintaining data about this class. The contents of the table, the data, may change over time depending on the events that occur in the organisation that affect the existence of specific projects. For example, new projects may be inititated, some projects may be completed and some projects may have certain characteristics about them changed (acquire a revised budget or have a new manager assigned to it). In each case, the impact of these organisational events must be reflected in the state of the data that we maintain so that the representation of data about our organisation is an accurate reflection

PROJECT-ID	PROJECT-TYPE	BUDGET	DOMESTIC-MARKET	START-DATE	MANAGER
A-2001	TACTICAL	400,000	T	31 January 1997	Able
A-1988	TACTICAL	380,000	F	20 January 1997	Baker
C-1031	STRATEGIC	800,000	T	3 February 1997	Able
C-875	OPERATIONAL	200,000	T	5 February 1997	Davis
B-9292	STRATEGIC	510,000	F	15 February 1997	Baker
D-1201	STRATEGIC	600,000	F	25 February 1997	Krull
D-3155	OPERATIONAL	150,000	F	1 March 1997	Krull
A-2010	STRATEGIC	1,000,000	T	10 March 1997	Charles
E-3221	MISSION	1,200,000	T	15 March 1997	Baker
F-4740	STRATEGIC	1,100,000	T	15 March 1997	Lineker
F-890	STRATEGIC	750,000	F	20 April 1997	Krull
F-1292	VISION	1,200,000	F	1 May 1997	Lineker

Figure 3.3. Project table.

Organizational events	Impact on table contents
A new project is initiated	A new row of data with values that describe this new project must be added to the table.
A project is completed (and therefore we are not interested in maintaining data about it)	The particular row of data that corresponds to this project must be removed from the table.
A project has its budget increased by 10%	The particular row of data that corresponds to this project must have the budget value revised accordingly.

Figure 3.4. Organisational events and impacts.

of what is actually going on in the organisation. Figure 3.4 shows examples of organisational events and their impact on the contents of the PROJECT table (Figure 3.3).

Several observations can be made about the PROJECT table (Figure 3.3) and its current set of 12 rows. Maintaining data about projects accurately means that the number of rows in the table may increase or decrease over time. Furthermore, the contents of a specific row may change in response to changing reality (e.g. revised project budget). This is not to suggest that the structure of the table itself is cast in stone. While it is necessary to carefully consider what the appropriate structure (property list) for the representation of a data class is, such an understanding might also change over time. This might come about in our example as a result of a new understanding about the PROJECT class, where we might wish to add a new attribute that describes it (such as the expected ending date of each project). This would necessitate the addition of a new column to the existing structure of the table and possibly updating each row of data to enter a value for this date for each project. However, it is important to note that the structure of Figure 3.3 supports an arbitrary number of rows. It does not change with a changing number of projects in the organisation.

3.2.2 Manipulating the Data

From the discussion in the earlier section, there are some basic manipulation requirements that are typical of database environments. Users need the ability to:

(a) retrieve data using arbitrarily specified criteria;
(b) add new rows of data to a table;
(c) delete single or multiple rows of data based on specifying deletion criteria;
(d) update single or multiple rows of data based on specifying update selection criteria.

Retrieval of data from a table requires that the users specify what attribute values should be displayed in the result (the target list of attributes), where the data is going to come from (the source table list) and the filtering criteria that will be applied to each row to see whether that row of data should be presented in the result (the criterion list). This specification is referred to as a database query. One of the more traditional approaches used for the expression of these queries is the use of the Structured Query Language (SQL). Relational database systems have adopted SQL as the de facto access language. We refer the reader to any standard book about relational database systems for a detailed coverage of SQL and its use.

In the context of SQL, it must be mentioned that many end users would argue that SQL is too cumbersome for the needs of DSS applications and that a visually driven approach is more sensible. An understanding of the essential structure of SQL queries is useful even when visually driven query interfaces are used since the same basic information must be provided by the user. Some knowledge about SQL, a relationally complete database-access language, will allow the user to accurately evaluate the limitations of a non-SQL interface.

3.2.3 The Visual Alternative

Several relational systems provide a visual form-based view of the data where retrieval specifications can be directly embedded to produce results. An example of such a system is Microsoft Access. The idea here is that if you can specify your criteria directly into a tabular structure, you can avoid the command language type of specification which is non-visual by nature. We use a few examples to demonstrate this approach.

Example 1

Retrieve all project IDs and their budgets: A query design screen presents the user with a blank palette onto which the user specifies all the source tables that are needed for the retrieval. The lower half of the palette is then used to carve out the structure of the result table along with any row-selection criteria, if necessary. In this example, by using the mouse the user can drag and drop into the result table those attributes of the PROJECT table that should appear in the result. No row-selection criteria are used here and hence all the rows from the source table appear in the result (Figure 3.5).

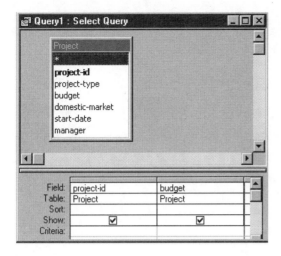

Figure 3.5. Visual querying.

Example 2

Retrieve project IDs and their managers for projects with budgets greater than $500,000 that started after 30 June 1997: In this example, there is an explicitly specified row-selection criterion that is to be used, (Figure 3.6). As is the case with the first example, the source table is specified: PROJECT. The drag-and-drop feature can now be used to specify two things: the attributes that must be displayed in the result and the row-selection criterion. The attributes to be displayed are marked with the check mark (using the mouse) against the row entitled 'Show' in the query design panel. The row-selection criterion which is based on specific values is entered against the row entitled 'Criteria'. The criteria are made up of two parts: a specific date value and a specific budget value. Both of these are entered as part of the criteria in the query design panel. However, since these attributes are not required to be displayed in the result, they are not checked in the row entitled 'Show' in the query panel. Only those rows from the project table that match the criteria of having a budget greater than $500,000 and a start date after 30 June 1997 will show up in the result table.

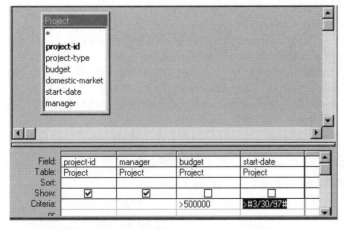

Figure 3.6. Visual querying with criteria.

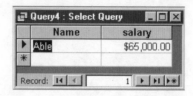

Figure 3.7. Visual querying with multiple tables.

Example 3

Retrieve the name and salary of the manager of project C-1031: This request involves the selection of data from two source tables. The two tables are related in the following way: the MANAGER in the PROJECT table is really the name of an employee (the NAME attribute in the EMPLOYEE table). Such equivalences can be expressed diagrammatically as shown in the query design panel in Figure 3.7. Now the result table can be fully specified by using the drag-and-drop feature and checking the attributes that should be displayed in the result as before. The criterion here is specified as a particular value for the project ID. Only one row in the PROJECT table has this particular value for project ID. Since the manager of the project in question is Able, the salary information must come from Able's row in the employee table. The table equivalence criterion shown on the diagram is able to link the two rows from their respective sources based on the same value for *MANAGER* and *NAME*: 'Able'. Now the salary for Able is retrieved and displayed as shown in the result panel (Figure 3.7). As an exercise, compare this visual approach to specifying the query with the corresponding SQL based approach.

As can be seen from these simple examples, the visual approach to specifying retrieval requests is more intuitive and easily understandable. However, the basic ideas that data are represented in tables and you need to know something about the structure of related tables still remain. Regardless of whether a visual, form-based approach or an SQL based approach is used, this basic information must be indicated for the system to perform the retrieval. Finally, note that every visually specified query has an SQL equivalent. As retrieval requests get more complicated, it becomes increasingly difficult to specify them using the visual, form-based approach. In such cases, the fall-back position is to use a language like SQL whose theoretical foundations make it a complete query specification language.

3.3 Object-Relational Database Systems

While relational systems play a very useful role in the management of data and have gained wide user acceptance, there is a growing recognition of the fact that the structures with which one works within a relational environment are constraining. Relational systems work well for a certain type of application where the data types involved are limited and simple, and envisioning data using a business forms analogy is convenient. However, in order to use relational systems effectively all data must be confined to the table structure and the user must then work with this structure to extract responses to queries. Sometimes, the correspondence between the meaning (*semantics*) of the data and the table structure used to represent it may not be straightforward resulting in the data-extraction process being complex.

The central notion behind an object-oriented approach is that a better fit is often necessary between how a user thinks about the application data and how the data is then represented in the database. This would enable a relatively simple mapping between a task requirement and the corresponding query specification. In order to facilitate this requirement in a database environment two important considerations are necessary. First, the data types that one is allowed to use in the application must be expanded beyond the simple types typically offered in a relational system. The use of such *complex types* as scanned images, geographic locations, payment schedules, etc. where the specific data need not be explicitly mapped into the basic types, is important. In fact, the user must be allowed to create an arbitrary number of data types based on the needs of the application. Recall that each data type has a set of allowable operations (manipulations) that can be performed on data of that type. When new data types are created, operations that are specific to that type can also be defined by the user, making query specification much easier. Many application domains that require database management also have the requirement that complex data be supported. These include financial investments, engineering design, geographical information systems, document management, etc. The second consideration is that the power of query languages used in relational systems must not be rejected for the sake of including complex data. Query languages in relational systems have a considerable track record in terms of their ability to perform well and have benefitted from over two decades of research. If the knowledge that we have gained from relational query languages can be retained while using complex data types, then data-oriented applications can benefit from greater versatility and more applicability. This is exactly what object-relational database systems attempt to do. A useful way to think about the capabilities of object-relational systems is to consider them as database systems that provide *necessary extensions* to relational database systems. The object-oriented features allow, among other things, the ability to deal with complex data. The relational features allow the use and development of query languages that have a long successful history.

Example 1: Nested Tables

Consider the following table definition to store data about persons and their dates of birth. This is a simple straightforward table structure that can be defined with any relational system discussed in the previous section. However, instead of name being a simple attribute, we might want to separate out the person's first, middle and last names explicit so that name is no longer a simple attribute. The structure of the table would appear as in Figure 3.8.

The structure is different from a traditional relational table in the following sense: the attribute *NAME* can be broken down into smaller components (first, middle and last), each of which contains textual data. In fact, we can think of *NAME* as a table structure itself which is embedded in a larger table called PERSON. We can define this aggregate as an attribute called *NAME*. The data type for this attribute is a reference to a table called

Attribute			Type of data
Name	First	Text	Name
	Middle	Text	
	Last	Text	
Date-of-birth			Date

Figure 3.8. Nested table structure: person.

NAME that contains the details of the components and their individual data types. Here the type is a reference to a table and not to the simple data types that we have discussed so far. This allows us to nest table structures within larger tables which is an important extension to relational systems.

Using SQL-type syntax, we can examine what a row of the table PERSON looks like (Figure 3.9).

select * from person;

	name			dob
	first	middle	last	
1	Charles	H	Spurgeon	04/19/1964

Figure 3.9. Querying a nested table.

We can use what is called a nested dot specification to see the details of the nested structure within the table as well. For example if we wanted to see the first names of all people in the person table, we could do that as shown in Figure 3.10.

select person.name.first from person;

	first
1	Charles

Figure 3.10. Using a nested dot specification for querying.

Note that the attribute list makes reference to an embedded attribute: the attribute *FIRST* that is part of an aggregate attribute *NAME* which is in the PERSON table.

Example 2: Functions

Another important characteristic of object relational systems is their ability to encapsulate behaviour (the manner by which data can change its values) as part of the definition of the structure itself. This is a fundamental object-oriented concept that has been built into these systems. For example, we might want to define a function (a stored definition for manipulating data) that can retrieve the information about a person's date of birth and use that to calculate the person's current age. We can call this function *AGE* and define it so that it performs the appropriate calculation if it is provided with a date-of-birth value. Once such a function is defined, it becomes part of the table structure itself and can be used in a query. Figure 3.11 shows the use of the *AGE* function using the SQL style of querying.

select *, age(dob) as age from person;

	name			dob	age
	first	middle	last		
1	Charles	H	Spurgeon	04/19/1964	34

Figure 3.11. Using functions.

Note that the AGE function needs a date-of-birth value to do the calculation and this is provided by saying that the value should be obtained from the *DOB* attribute that is contained in each row of the **PERSON** table. The resulting age value shows up in the results as a column of the table with the calculated value. Looking at the result, we cannot distinguish between a column like *DOB* that is part of the table definition and *AGE* that is a function. A function, once defined, becomes available to the user as if it was an attribute of the table.

Example 3: Using Sets of Data

In all our examples thus far, we have assumed that each attribute translates into a single value when we consider a row of data at the lowest level of detail. If we look at an attribute like *DOB*, in a row of data, it translates to specific values that correspond to the person who is represented in that row. However, consider an attribute called *SKILL*. A person may have many skills and we would want all of those skills to show up in the row of data for that person. The attribute *SKILL* is considered to be a *set attribute*. This means that it may contain a set of values instead of a single one. Figure 3.12 below illustrates this concept with the **SKILLEDEMP** table.

	name			dob	salary	skill
	first	middle	last			
1	Charles	M	Wesley	05/11/1987	3500.000	set(3) of varchar

1	Analysis
2	Research
3	Consult

Figure 3.12. Using sets: system-defined types.

The employee Wesley has three skills as is indicated in the upper portion of Figure 3.12. Details of what these skills are is shown in the lower portion of Figure 3.12. The idea of embedding set-oriented attributes can be extended further to contain sets of rows of data as well. In Figure 3.13, we show a **STUDENT** table where the set-of attribute is a reference to a set of *COURSES* and *GRADES* for a particular student.

name			dob	courses
first	middle	last		
Brown	M	Dragon	05/11/1987	set(2) of course_t

(row number 1)

	name	grade
1	Science	12.10000
2	Maths	12.10000

Figure 3.13. Using sets: user-defined types.

Example 4: Complex Data Types

Consider the structure of Figure 3.14 for the class PROJECT.

Attribute	Type description
Project_ID	Character
Budget	Integer
Start-Date	Date
End-Date	Date
Site	Point

Figure 3.14. Complex data types.

The first four attributes are readily understandable. The fifth attribute *SITE* marks the geographical location of the site where the particular project is being undertaken. While most of the structure looks like a traditional table definition that would be employed in a relational system, the attribute *SITE* is of a non-traditional type. Many applications where the geographical location of an object is important would find such a type to be useful. Data values for this attribute would consist of (x, y) pairs where the x and y values are distances from some reference point along the horizontal and vertical axes. A row from such a table would appear as follows:

a1028	500000	01/01/98	01/01/99	(354,200)

This row of data says that the project with ID 'a1028' has a budget of $500,000, a start date of 1 January 1998, an end date of 1 January 1999 and is located at a point (presumably on a map) at the location marked by (354,200). Recall that one of the important benefits of identifying the data type that you are working with is that the system can now apply type-specific operations on the data based on its type. In an object relational system, such as Informix, the user will be able to define the type '*point*' and, along with it, specify the operations and the logic that can be applied to all data of that type. An example of such an operation would be '*distance*' which would take as input two values of the type *point* and return a single value, which is the distance between the two points. The user could now include the function *DISTANCE* in a query, just like the inclusion of functions such as *AVERAGE* with values that are of the type *number*. The construction of such a query using the object relational system Informix is shown in Figure 3.15.

```
select pid, budget, distance(site, sp2Pnt(175, 37)) as
Distance from project;
```

	pid	budget	distance
1	a1028	500000	242.095022666721
2	b1028	600000	76.2167960491649
3	c1028	700000	267.944024005015
4	d1028	800000	672.554830478527

Figure 3.15. Functions with complex data types.

The function *DISTANCE* makes reference to two points: the location of the project as indicated by the value of the attribute *SITE* and a specific point on a map indicated by its *x, y* co-ordinates. The prefix '*sp2Pnt*' is how Informix notifies the system that this is a value of a particular type ('*point*'). The result shows the distance between this point and each of the projects.

3.3.1 Using a Visually Oriented Approach

As mentioned in the case of relational systems, some object relational systems also offer a visual alternative to constructing queries. The visualisation approach taken by Visionary, the companion to the Informix object relational database system, is demonstrated in this section.[2] Instead of taking a forms-oriented view of the data, Visionary allows the user to think of query definition as describing how data flows into a result. The components to create the flow are tables, functions, etc. If we revisit Example 2 where we used the function age to display the ages of employees, the visualisation of the query is shown as Case 1 in Figure 3.16.

The table PERSON provides the input date that is passed through the function *AGE* producing the result. The example for calculating distances between points is a little more complicated and we show the visualisation as Case 2 in Figure 3.16. Note that, in this example, the co-ordinates of the reference site (175,37) are first converted into a spatial data type by the function sp2Pnt. This places one part of the input into the distance function. The table project provides the site-location data into the distance function which in turns produces the result shown in Example 4.

Visualisation is a powerful tool that places the utility of versatile systems in the hands of even a casual user. A great deal of functionality is obtainable from the use of such interfaces and it is worth the time and effort involved in investigating its availability with any potentially useful system.

3.4 Spreadsheets

Spreadsheets are very powerful decision support tools that can potentially support a wide range of decision-making activities. The format used to represent data in a spreadsheet is intuitively appealing, which probably explains the widespread acceptance of the platform. The paradigm of using columns and rows is similar to the relational approach to envisioning data. However, the appeal of the spreadsheet comes from its ability for instant expression evaluation. In other words, data stored using the column and row

[2] The examples in this book use an early release of Visionary.

Case 1: Functions with simple types

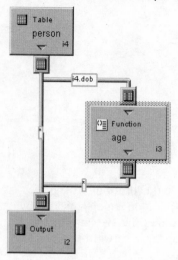

Case 2: Functions with complex types

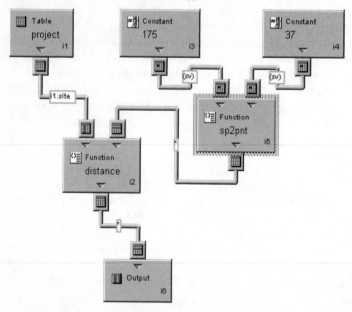

Figure 3.16. Visual querying.

format can be manipulated by directly expressing manipulation rules on the spreadsheet that yield the result with no further requests from the user. It is precisely because of this feature that spreadsheets can serve as a vital platform for the modelling aspect of DSS design. We will focus our attention in this section on the ability of spreadsheet environments to support modelling-related activities.

The spreadsheet allows a variety of models to be represented using the row and column structure of spreadsheets. Tools and technologies made available within the spreadsheet not only allow it to support different decision-making phases like Intelligence, Design,

Choice and Review but also different decision-making styles. These tools support decision making in contexts with varying degrees of structure. Most spreadsheet environments have integrated graphing capabilities that provide visual support to modelling activities that can be useful for conducting analyses based on varying problem assumptions – a necessary activity in many decision-making processes.

3.4.1 An Example: Sales Forecasting

To focus on the modelling capabilities of a spreadsheet environment, we develop a simple modelling application using a Microsoft Excel environment. Our objective in this section is to demonstrate model building and evaluation along with graphical imperatives that make such applications more useful. It is not our intent to demonstrate all the possible features that are available in a spreadsheet platform.

Consider an application where we have access to historical sales data and want to use it as a basis to generate sales forecasts. Specifically, Figure 3.17 shows sales figures for the past 12 time periods. The data may be directly entered in a spreadsheet exactly as shown in Figure 3.17 using two columns and as many rows as necessary to capture the data.

The data may be selected and displayed graphically in a traditional manner using the graphing capabilities of the spreadsheet. The resulting display is shown in Figure 3.18.

The modelling element of this exercise is to generate a sales forecast using this data. There are many different ways to generate forecasts. We will use a method that involves the generation of a trend line for this data. Basically what this means is that we want to construct a straight line that best represents the historical data that we have. We can then extend this trend line into the future to examine what the sales figures might look like in future time periods should the present trend continue. The line itself can be described in

Period	Sales (in 000s)
1	22
2	32
3	38
4	27
5	44
6	48
7	38
8	45
9	55
10	66
11	62
12	45

Figure 3.17. Sales data in a spreadsheet.

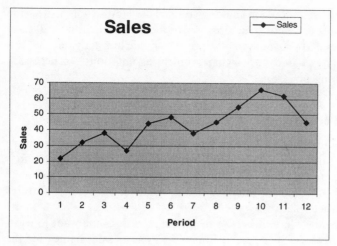

Figure 3.18. Graphing sales data.

terms of its slope and its intercept – this constitutes the forecasting model. Further, the degree to which the trend fits the data can be expressed in terms of a value that ranges from 0 to 1. A value of 1 means that the line fits the data perfectly. This is known as the coefficient of determination of the line usually denoted by R^2.

Generating the best trend line involves the use of a statistical model that takes the historical sales data as input and generates the trend line. The data is manipulated as per the rules of the model resulting in the specification of a trend line that best fits the data. Such a model is a built-in feature of the spreadsheet environment and can be invoked to act on data that is in the spreadsheet. The information that the user needs to specify includes the location of the data on the spreadsheet and a specification of how far into the future the trend line needs to be extended. This can all be done using the graphical interface and by pointing and clicking with the mouse. The result of applying this built-in model on the data results in a trend line that is shown in the resulting chart (Figure 3.19).

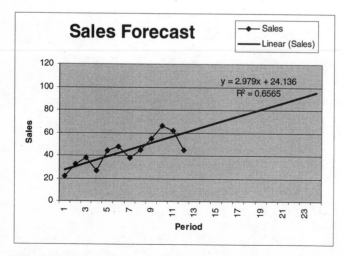

Figure 3.19. Modelling a trend line.

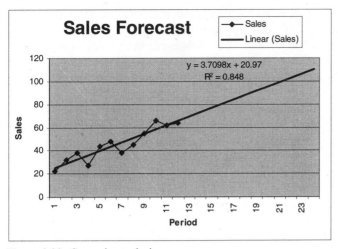

Figure 3.20. Scenario analysis.

The chart itself is displayed right on the spreadsheet that contains the data. The following are worth noting:

- The original graph of the data has now been modified to show the trend line that is superimposed on the graph. The line extends to several periods beyond the data as specified by the user.
- The built-in model guarantees that this is the line that best fits the data.
- The description of the line is presented on the graph in the form of an equation for the line.
- The fit between the trend line and the data is indicated by the R^2 value of 0.6565 that is shown on the graph.

The real power of modelling is the ability of the user to conduct ad hoc analyses on the results. For example, consider the situation where the user wants to examine the sensitivity of the trend line to changes in the historical data. Specifically, assume that the user wants to investigate the effects of better sales in the last time period on the trend line. This can be done in two ways: the data in the appropriate location in the spreadsheet can be manually updated; alternatively, the appropriate data point can be moved by dragging and dropping it with the mouse at a new location on the graph. Doing this immediately produces a revised trend line along with the revised specification and R^2 value, all of which are shown in Figure 3.20. We use this example to demonstrate some critical aspects of the modelling process and how spreadsheets can support them.

3.5 The Role of Visualisation Technologies

In many of our examples in this chapter, we have made references to a visually oriented mechanism to interact with an application. Many basic design technologies provide such an interface to allow users to engage with the system in an intuitively appealing manner. Hence, examples with spreadsheet, relational and object relational environments include such an approach to interaction in addition to more traditional interaction modes. In this section, we examine a particular system that attempts to provide powerful functionality throughout the modelling process in a visually oriented manner. We offer this as an example of what the possibilities for visually driven modelling are.

Clementine (Integral Solutions Limited, 1996) is a data-mining toolkit whose visual-programming interface allows accessing, manipulating and experimenting with data, and testing out hypotheses. The user selects, manipulates and links together icons to form different scenarios. Icons could connect to databases, manipulate and derive new data, build rules from data, plot graphs, histograms and data webs, regress on data, equalise distributions, etc. Icons are selected from a palette, placed on a drawing board and connected using arrows to form modelling scenarios. These scenarios are executed to produce output in the form of rules, predictions, graphs, models, etc. Clementine supports most parts of the modelling life cycle well. We demonstrate some of these features by using the sales-forecasting example from the previous section. The fundamental issues that need to be addressed are:

- How are the data requirements for the application defined?
- How does the user define and select data manipulation models that will be applied to the data?
- How does the user specify the way in which results will be displayed?

The approach that Clementine takes is to offer the use a blank slate – a palette – on which building blocks are located as icons by the user. These building blocks correspond to data, models and outputs. By linking these icons with directed arcs, the user is able to specify a flow model of arbitrary complexity. Thus, what the user does is to use a collection of nodes connected by arrows to describe the task at hand. In our sales-forecasting example, we need to specify the historical sales data as input, the application of the regression model to produce the trend line and the display of the results in an appropriate manner. Figure 3.21 shows a sample layout of the relevant icons for our problem.

The nodes and arrows are used to indicate the components that describe the problem at hand. We know that the data that needs to be input refers to the historical sales data. This is indicated by choosing an icon from the selection panel (bottom half of Figure 3.21) which indicates what the data source is and providing it with a label. In this case, the data actually come from a spreadsheet that is linked to the palette through an Open Data Base Connectivity (ODBC) connection (an example of a platform integration tool). This node is provided with the label 'trend'. The data can be displayed if desired using a tabular output. This is indicated by the node marked table that is linked to the data source. The node 'type' specifies what the input and output variables in the model are: *TIME PERIOD* and *SALES* respectively in our example. Finally, the node marked 'Sales' specifies that the execution of a regression model (used to generate a trend line), which is selected from a choice set from the panel below, should produce a model-execution result entitled *SALES*. Now the palette contains a complete visually specified execution sequence. When executed, a model instance is created which is indicated as the icon marked 'E Sales' (see top right of the panel). This is really an equation that is generated as a result of executing the regression model using the particular dataset as input. A forecasting task can now be specified by using this model instance as an icon placed on the palette. This is shown in Figure 3.22. Here the desired output is indicated by selecting a graph display from the selection panel producing the result shown in Figure 3.23.

The purpose of this example is to show one method by which powerful modelling applications can be approached through mechanisms that are driven visually from specification to display of the results. A platform such as Clementine contains a suite of commonly used models for manipulation purposes. If a task at hand can be well served by

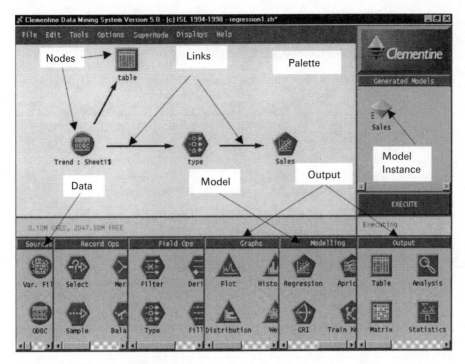

Figure 3.21. The Clementine palette.

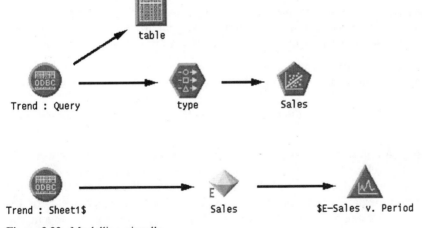

Figure 3.22. Modelling visually.

a particular model offered, then visual modelling can be employed by the user using input data from an arbitrary source.

3.6 Integration

Throughout our discussions, we have emphasised the fact that typical decision support applications need to be concerned with data, models, solvers and presentation. Various sections of this chapter have referred to design environments that might service some of these requirements well (at the expense of others). For example, database environments

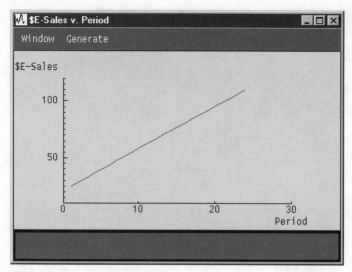

Figure 3.23. Modelling results.

are built to provide efficient data services but limited modelling services. Automation is the technology that allows two separate application components to communicate with each other. The Component Object Model (COM) is a methodology for this communication and allows the building of stand-alone components. COM specifies the interface that allows different software to interact. Apart from these two types of environments, any environment where automation is enabled is potentially capable of being linked with other environments which are also automation enabled. Automation-enabled environments provide a number of services that can be reused in other environments, for example:

- Spreadsheets built with Excel and Lotus 123 provide modelling and graphing services.
- Database-management systems like Oracle, Access and Informix provide database services.
- Word processors like Word, WordPerfect, etc., provide word processing and publishing services.

When developing an application, it is important to consider whether components of the application can be developed in environments which are strong in certain types of services with a view toward integrating these components into a finished design product. It might be useful to develop the data aspects of an application in a database environment and the modelling aspects in a spreadsheet environment and link the two components together in the final delivered product.

3.6.1 Examples

The key premise behind integration is to think of design in terms of components. Figure 3.24 shows a hypothetical example of what we may try to achieve.

Consider the regression example that we have used in an earlier section of this chapter. Historical sales data may exist in a table as part of a database application. In order to generate a forecasting application, using a regression model applied to this data, we want to utilise the modelling capabilities of a spreadsheet platform. The integration strategy consists of using the modelling capability of the spreadsheet platform without having to

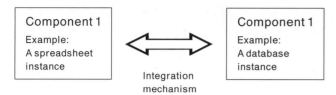

Figure 3.24. Integration of components.

enter the data explicitly into the spreadsheet. Instead, we want to reference the database application as the source for the data from within the spreadsheet. Further, we want to do this in a manner that maintains this link between the two environments in a dynamic manner. What this means is that if there are any changes made to the data in the database application, the link ensures that those updates are reflected in the modelling application. We show a series of screen shots below that show the process for accomplishing this using Microsoft Access and Microsoft Excel as the database and spreadsheet platforms.

3.6.2 Defining the Source of Data in an Excel Spreadsheet

Figure 3.25 shows the definition of the source of data within the spreadsheet environment. The particular database, system, the name of the database and the table which contains the data are all specified. The opportunity to link to data subsets with a query interface also exist.

The particular location of the data on the spreadsheet can be specified by indicating the cell location for entering data. It is important to note that the data (shown in Figure 3.26) in the spreadsheet is dynamically linked to the database. This means that any change to the data in the database will automatically update the entry in the spreadsheet thereby ensuring that the data in the two environments are always consistent.

The data in the spreadsheet can now be used as input for any sort of modelling exercise. In our example, we could apply the built-in regression modelling capability in Excel to generate a graphic display of forecasted sales figures by conducting a trend analysis.

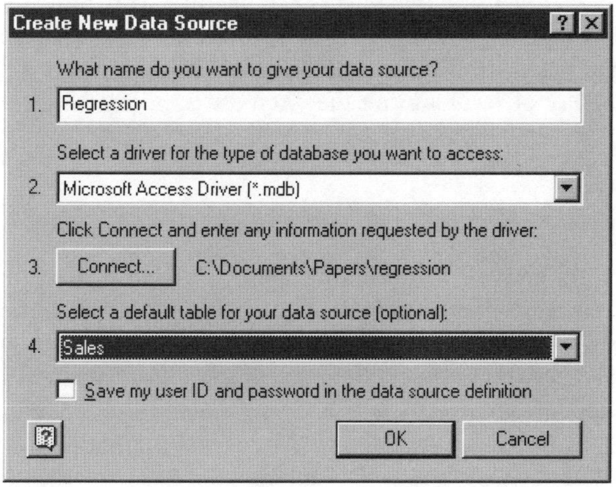

Figure 3.25. Sourcing of the data.

Period	Sales
1	22
2	32
3	38
4	27
5	44
6	48
7	38
8	45
9	55
10	66
11	62
12	64

Figure 3.26. The spreadsheet view.

3.6.3 Using the Database Environment as the Dominant Platform

In some cases, it is possible that the dominant application platform is the database environment. In other words, the database platform is used to look at results, display graphs and examine alternative scenarios. Continuing the previous example, the results of the regression modelling exercise could now be linked back to a display window within the Access environment. We now show how this is done (Figure 3.27).

Linking the contents of a spreadsheet dynamically to the database platform starts with specifying the region in the spreadsheet that needs to be linked. The region can be highlighted with the mouse and prepared for copying.

The appropriate database display window is opened and the copied portion of the spreadsheet is linked into the display window using the 'Paste Link' feature. This provides a dynamic link to the results of the modelling exercise in the spreadsheet as shown in Figure 3.28. This is particularly useful when we want to utilise the modelling power of a spreadsheet but want to drive the display of results using the database application.

3.7 Conclusion

In this chapter we have outlined a framework for thinking about designing decision support applications. The fundamental conceptual components consist of the interaction between data, their methods of manipulation (models and solvers) and the interaction between the user and the application. These conceptual components must work their way into the implemented system. The chapter surveys some useful implementation ideas by making reference to some software platforms that could serve as design building blocks. Specifically, we discussed relational database systems, object relational database systems, spreadsheet environments, visualisation technologies and integration technologies. In the

Figure 3.27. Selecting a portion of the spreadsheet.

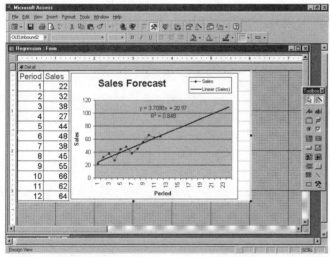

Figure 3.28. The view from the database form.

next few chapters, we turn to complete examples of implemented systems using some of the ideas that have been developed here.

References

Chappell, D. (1996) *Understanding ActiveX and OLE: A Guide for Developers and Managers*, Microsoft Press, Redmond, Washington.

Codd, E. F. (1970) A relational model of data for large shared data banks, *Communications of the ACM*, 13 June 1970, 377–387.

Integral Solutions Limited (1998) *Clementine User's Guide*, Basingstoke, UK.

Rob, P. and Coronel, C. (1997) *Database Systems: Design, Implementation, and Management*, International Thomson Publishing Company, Cambridge, Massachussetts.

Stonebraker, M. and Brown, P. (1999) *Object Relational DBMSs: Tracking the Next Great Wave*, Morgan Kaufmann Publishers, Inc., San Francisco, California.

Winston, W. L. and Albright, S. C. (1997) *Practical Management Science: Spreadsheet Modelling and Applications*, Duxbury Press, Belmont, California.

DISCUSSION QUESTIONS

1. Discuss the conceptual component layer of the DSS architecture proposed in this chapter in the context of technologies that you are familiar with.
2. Identify data, models, solvers and interfaces with respect to a decision support application in an organisational context of your choice.
3. Describe how you would implement a decision support system of your choice using spreadsheets as the driving technology. Keep in mind the need for supporting the various components in the Conceptual Component layer (data, models, solvers, interfaces).
4. Describe how you would implement the same system as in #3 using an object relational database system as the driving technology. Again, be sure to address the requirements from the Conceptual Component layer.
5. What are the advantages and disadvantages of using (a) spreadsheets and (b) object relational systems as the main implementation platforms for DSS design?

4
Modularity and Integration: An Application in Retailing[1]

4.1 Introduction

In this chapter we explore in some detail the example of the retailing situation that was briefly described in Chapter 1. This brings into focus some of the concepts that we have described in the previous two chapters. The application describes the design and development of a prototype decision support system built for a large multinational consumer-goods manufacturing and marketing company. Analysis of the marketing environment and the role of promotions, which leads to the identification of the critical decisions that needed to be supported, are discussed. Diverse data needs and suitable models to analyse the data are of particular interest. The important principle that is demonstrated in this chapter is the necessity to bring together the capabilities from different development environments under a single-application umbrella. The focus in this chapter is on integrating data-specific needs that are addressed in a data-management environment and modelling specific needs that are addressed in a spreadsheet environment. Further, the display capabilities of these two environments are leveraged to present data to the user in meaningful ways. The approach that we take enables us to develop the various aspects of the application in modular fashion, taking advantage of the capabilities offered by separate development environments.

4.2 The Organisational Context and Associated Problems

There has been an explosive increase in the amount of raw data available to decision makers dealing with marketing-related decisions in recent years. Developments, such as supermarket scanners, hand-held computers, smart cards, etc., have made possible the rapid gathering and processing of large amounts of valuable data. UPC scanners in supermarkets capture data about the prices and movements of every item sold as part of the normal operations. Such data gathered from multiple retail outlets is available from data vendors such as Nielsen in an easy-to-use form at several levels of aggregation. Scanner panel data provides coverage of products purchased, promotion exposure, television viewing and household characteristics at the level of individual households. The possibility of mining the extensive census data using geographical information systems (GIS) software for improving marketing decisions have also been explored. Some of this data is usually available from the public domain. Other data, especially that at the level of individual stores, can be purchased from third parties.

[1] This chapter is adapted from Davis, J. G., and Sundaram, D. (1995) PETAPS: A prototype decision support system for consumer product marketing and promotion, *European Journal of Operational Research*, **87**, 247–256.

The rapid availability of large amounts of data has prompted the creation of a variety of response models that use such data. The development and use of appropriate and informative models of brands of products using scanner and related data has been pioneered by Blattberg and Wisniewski (1986) among others.

The application discussed in this context integrates the diverse data available to promotion managers in a large multinational consumer-goods manufacturing and marketing company, with suitable promotion-response models using a variety of software tools to prototype a system that will assist the managers in making near-optimal decisions in the area of product promotions. Consistent with the DSS approach, the system is designed to be easy to use and to be 'driven' by the managers.

4.2.1 Overall Market System Structure

The market system applicable to the focal firm has been modelled along the lines suggested by Little (1975a). The viewpoint is that of the manufacturer and marketer operating in a consumer-product market. This model as shown in Figure 4.1 has five principal elements, namely manufacturer, competitors, retailers, consumers and the general environment.

The manufacturer affects the final customer by the product itself with its function and quality and by price, advertising, various promotional devices such as coupons and samples, package appearance and function, and the assortment of sizes and packages offered. The manufacturer affects the retailer by its sales force and promotional activity such as temporary price reductions. The retailer affects the consumer by placement of product, price, special promotions, display and by media advertising. Environmental factors affect the consumer, including seasonality and economic trends. Consumer sales affect the retailer with respect to stocking and displaying the product. Similarly, the retailer presents the manufacturer with a distribution and sales situation to which the manufacturer reacts. Competitive manufacturers enter the system by offering competitive products and brands with essentially the same control variables, but they are more likely to hinder rather than aid the sales of the brand under consideration.

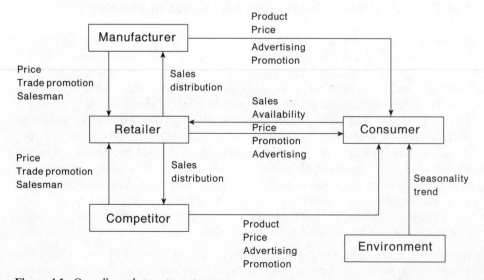

Figure 4.1. Overall market system structure.

4.2.2 Decision Making in the Area of Product Promotions

Based on extensive discussions with key decision makers and other participants and a survey of the literature, the following sequential decisions were identified as being critical in the context of product promotion.

1. Selection of products that need to be promoted.
2. Selection of retailers where the promotion needs to be conducted.
3. Selection of the types of promotion that are most effective for the chosen product–retailer combination.
4. Determining the optimal spending for the promotion.

Product-promotion managers typically used simple rules of thumb and heuristics like percentage of profits to decide on how much to spend on a particular promotion. Moreover, the strong bargaining position enjoyed by the retailers enabled them to virtually dictate the cost of in-store promotions. Since no cost–benefit analysis was being done, there was no clear basis by which the firm could negotiate the cost of promotion with the retailer. Hence there was a need for a system that will help the promotions manager to take informed decisions based on the impacts of previous promotions: decisions that could be justified and are cost-effective. It was to meet this perceived need that the application, Promotions Evaluation Tracking and Planning System (PETAPS), was designed.

4.3 The Design Approach

The design of PETAPS was centred around the four key sequential decisions referred to earlier. PETAPS has an open architecture that allows for modifications over time such as changes to the existing models, addition of new models and incorporation of new features. A brief description of the decision-making process using PETAPS is provided.

4.3.1 The Decision-making Process Using PETAPS

PETAPS is a system that requires active participation of the manager in making the decisions. It actively assists the manager in making decisions based on graphical representation of historical data as well as analyses using appropriate models. The process by which the decisions are reached using PETAPS is explained below.

4.3.1.1 Selection of Product–Retailer Combination for Promotion

The selection of a specific product to be promoted and the specific retailer where the product will be promoted are interrelated. This selection could be based on any user-specified criteria. In this instance the user specified that declining sales over a period of time would be an appropriate indicator. The system also provides the user with the means to define the percentage decline that is significant. This assists in filtering out, for the user's inspection, those products at different retailers that have declined in sales beyond the level specified by the user. The parameters used for the selection of product and retailer are:

1. Period of comparison.
2. Sales volume, dollar value.
3. Percent decline above which to monitor.

The period of comparison could be current week with previous week or current 2 weeks with previous 2 weeks or current 4 weeks with previous 4 weeks. The comparison could be by sales volume or by dollar value. Also, the change monitored could be absolute change in sales or market-share change. The analysis could be industry-wide (analysing products that are declining in the total market) or store-wide (analysing products that are declining at a particular retail store).

4.3.1.2 Selection of the Type of Promotion that is Most Effective

The focus on a specific promotion type for further analysis is dependent on having knowledge about effective retailer–product pairs. In other words, the user needs to know which retailers and products to focus on in order to rethink promotion-related spending of various types. Such information can be presented graphically or using a business form in such a way that it highlights areas to concentrate on.

A graphical view helps in the identification of promotions that were most effective; that is, the promotion that gives rise to the maximum sales. It also assists in finding the effect of price reduction on sales, effect of promotion along with price reduction on sales, promotions that have long-ranging effects, etc. A business forms-oriented view helps in the selection of an area of promotion to focus on and link that selection to more sophisticated analysis.

4.3.1.3 Determining the Optimal Spending for the Promotion

Two models to help determine the optimal level of promotional spending for a selected product–retailer combination for a particular type of promotion were considered. These models can assist the user in gauging the likely sales for a particular promotional intensity as well as the optimal amount to spend for a promotion. The models used are:

(a) The ADBUDG model proposed by Professor John Little (Lilien, 1986; Little, 1969; 1975a; 1975b; 1979).
(b) A modified version of the promotional model used by Mobil Corporation (Lilien, 1986; Rao and Lilien, 1972).

These models require the user to input various parameters such as minimum sales without promotion and maximum possible sales with maximum promotion. These values can be modified by the user so that the model can be fine-tuned to reflect specific conditions.

4.3.2 The ADBUDG Model

The ADBUDG model is based on decision calculus developed by Little (1975a) and it enables the managers to structure their experience into a formal model that is then used in subsequent decision making. Apart from the user input it utilises considerable historical data. The predicted sales and profit versus promotional spending graph as in Figure 4.2 can be used to decide on the optimal spending level which would be at the point at which profit and/or sale is maximum.

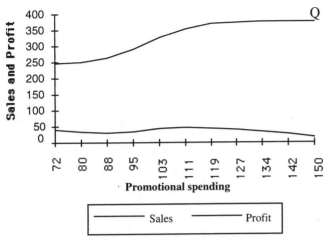

Figure 4.2. Results from model-based analysis.

The ADBUDG Model can be expressed in the form of the following equation:

$$Q = a_0 + (a_1 - a_0) \times (X^{a_2}/(a_3^{a_2} + X^{a_2}))$$

where Q = sales predicted by the model; a_0 = sales with no promotion; a_1 = maximum possible sales with maximum promotion; X = promotional spending.

When promotional spending is varied with respect to sales the equation yields an S-shaped curve of the kind depicted in Figure 4.2. That is, at small values of promotional spending promotion works poorly, either because the customer is not attracted enough or the retailer is not pushing the product in the market. In the middle-range response to promotional spending rises fast until a plateau is reached where the customer finds the promotion attractive financially or otherwise and the retailer is also actively promoting the product. a_2 and a_3 are parameters that are varied by the system to get the S curve that best fits the historical data for the product in question using the R_2 statistic. The user can override this automatic (system) selection of a_2 and a_3 parameters and input those parameter values that he/she thinks are appropriate for the product. The user has the goodness-of-fit index, namely the value of R_2, as a guide in the selection of the parameters. The profit curve is generated using the list price and standard costs data in the database.

4.3.3 The Mobil Corporation Promotion Model

This is a multiplicative model and is analogous to the ADBUDG model. The main difference is the inclusion of a 'Reach' variable which represents the proportion of the total number of consumers that might be reached by a particular type of promotion. The model can be expressed in the following equation form:

$$Q = a_0 + (X^{a_2}/(a_3^{a_2} + X^{a_2})) \times R \times (1 - m) \times G$$

where Q = sales predicted by the model; a_0 = sales with no promotion; X = promotional spending; R = reach of the promotion; m = current market share; G = total market volume.

This model also generates an S-shaped curve similar to the one generated by the ADBUDG model. a_2 and a_3 are parameters that are varied by the system to get the S curve that best fits the historical data for the product in question using the R^2 statistic. The user can override this automatic system selection of a_2 and a_3 parameters and input those parameter values that are defined as more appropriate for the product. The user has a goodness-of-fit index, namely the value of R_2, as a guide in the selection of the parameters. The profit curve as in the previous case is generated using the list price and standard cost data in the database, provided by the firm.

The user is given the freedom to change the various parameters of the models and examine the effects of these changes. In other words, the user has the ability to carry out sensitivity or what-if analysis on the models. An important component built into the process of modelling is the assessment of the model's ability to replicate historical data. This assessment involves the use of goodness-of-fit statistics that provides a quantitative analysis of the difference between the set of model predictions and the set of historical values of the dependent variable in the model. An example of this is assessing the difference between the forecasted sales and historical sales that had occurred for a particular value of promotional spending. The goodness-of-fit statistic used in this case was the coefficient of determination (R^2) (Fotheringham and Knudsen, 1987) and is of the form:

$$R^2 = \frac{\sum_{i=1}^{n}(y_i - \bar{y})^2 - \sum_{i=1}^{n}(y_i - \hat{y})^2}{\sum_{i=1}^{n}(y_i - \bar{y})^2}$$

where y is the mean of the known (historical) dataset; n is the number of observations; y is the mean of the dataset replicated by the model.

The statistic R^2 ranges between 0 and 1. If the model replicates the known dataset value for value perfectly, R^2 will be equal to 1. The value of R^2 can be interpreted as the proportion of the variance of y explained by the model.

The use of the models in PETAPS is inspired by Little (1975b). The users of the system are provided with the flexibility of choosing the more appropriate model and to vary the model parameters to examine the extent to which the sales function for a particular product at a particular retail store matches the user's intuitive understanding of the product sales response to different levels of promotion. Thus, the users are able to parametrise the models to the point they feel comfortable with the representation. Our initial user trials have indicated that this feature contributes to greater micro-level learning on the part of promotion managers regarding specific and general market response to promotions. In case they are uncomfortable with this option (especially if they are new to the job or inexperienced), they can resort to the unparametrised version established with available historical data. PETAPS is thus designed to be a decision support and learning tool.

The system can assist the company in selecting a product to promote, a retailer to promote the product in, the type of promotion that is most effective and the optimal amount that should be spent on the promotion. The system has been implemented in such a way that the result of one decision becomes the input to the next decision and so on. This reduces the need for the user to remember the results of the previous decision phases.

The following assumptions were made in the modelling of the problem:

(a) Sales may exist without any promotions.

(b) There may be a limit to the level of sales, no matter how much is spent on the promotion.

(c) In general, sales will be higher when promotional expenses are higher.

4.4 Structure of PETAPS

The three major components of PETAPS – the database and database management software, the model base and model-base-management software, and the user interface – are discussed below.

4.4.1 Database Issues

To support the decisions identified, the data required were spread in different systems and in different formats. The primary data sources were:

(1) Nielsen's INF*ACT Workstation Scan Track databases – these data are from scanners at the point of sale, namely retail stores. The INF*ACT databases had sales data about package sales, cash sales, etc. for each retailer, for different products and for different periods (104 weeks in total).

(2) Database managed by the organisation in their enterprise data-management environment. The data required from this source were product cost details such as list price and standard cost for a product at different points in time.

(3) Details of all promotional activities undertaken by the firm. Historical data regarding the various costs involved in the promotion of a particular product at a particular retailer using a particular type of promotion were extracted from paper documents.

Since all three sources of data needed to be integrated on the period/time dimension, an application specific data management environment was created. The data aspects of this application are developed using the Access DBMS.

4.4.2 Modelling Issues

As mentioned earlier, the ADBUDG and MOBIL models were chosen for the model base component of PETAPS. These models have been tested in similar consumer-goods markets and found to be useful. The models were implemented in an environment that allowed ease of implementation, ease of change, a facility for 'what-if' questions to be addressed to the model and good presentation graphics. Given that spreadsheet packages offered these capabilities and were familiar to managers, they were used to store and manage the models. The Excel spreadsheet environment was the choice that was made for this purpose. Excel supports a wide range of mathematical, financial and statistical models, offers excellent graphics facility and provides for good integration between different applications. The Solver facility of Excel was very useful in making the system automatically select the a_2 and a_3 parameters for a specific product–retailer-type of promotion combination. The ability to exchange data dynamically with the database facility was also very useful in making the system appear seamless to the user. The models were implemented in Excel in such a way that the user has complete control and can modify them to suit his/her requirements.

4.4.3 User Interface Issues

A user interface that users would be comfortable with and could learn to use within a short

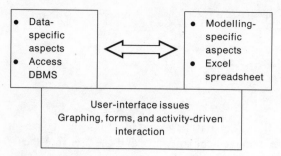

Figure 4.3. General Application Structure.

span of time was an important consideration. Besides, the user interface had to provide facilities for integrating the different components of the DSS. Both Access and Excel provide useful interface mechanisms that we utilised in designing the system. Access has a useful forms-oriented display feature that can be quickly designed to present data to the user in an informative manner. Further, the facility to make parts of the form active by using its facility for 'drill-down' was taken advantage of. This was particularly helpful in designing a system where the user can navigate with ease from the macro-level (analysis at retailer level) to the micro-level (analysis at period level for a particular product in a particular retailer). The ability to exchange data dynamically between the database and the spreadsheet was used to seamlessly integrate the unique features of the two environments. The spreadsheet environment offers a powerful graphing facility that is useful to display the kind of information that we modelled in this application. The general structure of the PETAPS system is shown in Figure 4.3.

4.5 A sample session on PETAPS

PETAPS is an interactive system. The user is able to fine-tune the system to suit the environment. The system obtains from the user parameters like analysis by product (units) or dollars, store-wide or industry-wide analysis, period of analysis and the rate of decline of the sales beyond which to analyse. Based on the environmental parameters, PETAPS supports the decisions identified.

4.5.1 Selection of Products and Retailers for Promotion

The basic table of data that drives the application is the MARKET table. Figure 4.4 shows the structure and an excerpt of the data that is contained in this table. The important attributes of the table are the following:

Market: the specific retail outlet where the sale occurs
Product: the particular product that is sold
Period: the time period for which the sales figures are reported
Cost: various cost-related data
Sales: the sale quantity
Promotype: the type of promotion that was conducted during the period
Promoamt: the amount spent on a particular promotion
List Price: the price at which the product is sold in the store
Stdcost: the cost to manufacture the product

Conversion: some products are sold in batches or cartons that can contain more than one unit of product.

To help the user choose the product and the retailer to be considered for a promotion, PETAPS displays useful data using a sales-decline analysis form, as shown in Figure 4.5.

Market : Table

Field Name	Data Type
MARKET	Text
PRODUCT	Text
PERIOD	Date/Time
SALES	Number
PROMOTYPE	Number
PROMOAMT	Number
LISTPRICE	Number
STDCOST	Number
CONVERSION	Number

Market : Table

MARKET	PRODUCT	PERIOD	SALES	PROMOTYPE	PROMOAMT	LISTPRICE	STDCOST	CONVERSION
FT	Q5423	7/25/92	116.4	1	26.77	23.46	17.94	12
FT	Q5423	8/1/92	100	2	19.17	23.46	17.94	12
FT	Q5423	8/8/92	91	3	18.2	23.46	17.94	12
WWG	B2611	2/8/92	379	1	81.11	21.83	16.69	12
WWG	B2611	2/15/92	476	2	84.89	21.83	16.69	12
WWG	B2611	2/22/92	463	3	85.76	21.73	16.61	12
WWG	B2611	2/29/92	489	4	74.75	21.83	16.69	12
WWG	B2611	3/7/92	406.3	0	0	21.93	16.77	12
WWG	B2611	3/14/92	433	6	70.95	21.73	16.61	12
WWG	B2611	3/21/92	378	7	61.64	21.62	16.54	12
WWG	B2611	3/28/92	411.9	8	62.08	21.52	16.46	12

Figure 4.4. The basic data table.

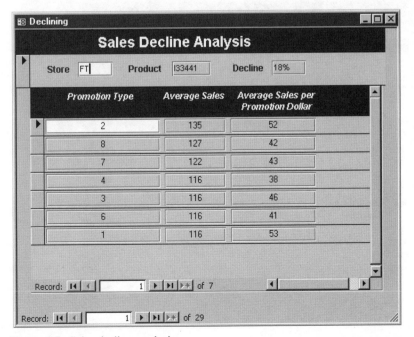

Figure 4.5. Sales-decline analysis.

This is a form that displays the percent decline in sales for a particular product at a particular retailer in descending order. The user can now make an informed decision regarding the selection of a product to promote and retailer to promote it in. The form also displays the various promotions that were used for one retailer–product pair at a time. Since it is ordered in a way that displays the greatest percentage decline first, these pairs are presented in a suggested order of importance for the user. The user can scroll through all product–retailer pairs using this form. For each pair, the specific promotion-related pattern is displayed.

4.5.2 Form-design Considerations

For every combination of retailer and product, there are one or more promotions. It is useful to think of this situation as a main form that contains retailer–product combinations (and related information) and a subform that contains the associated promotion details. Each of the forms are defined in terms of their format, the content (via typical queries) and the linking attributes between the two. The main form is based on the declining query and the subform is based on the promotions query. We link the main form and subform through linking the store and product columns of the declining and promotions queries. Figure 4.6 shows how these considerations are built into the design of the form.

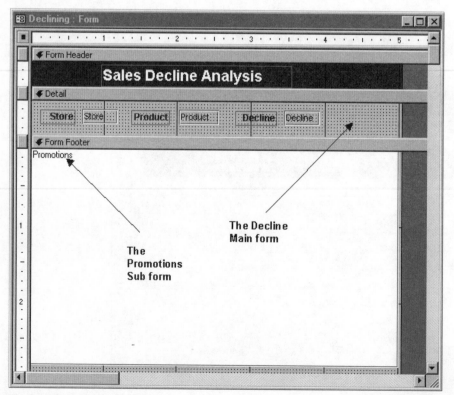

Figure 4.6. Form-design issues.

The first action

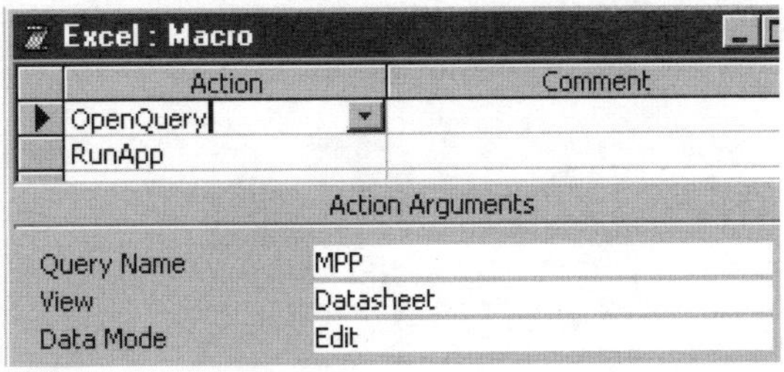

The second action

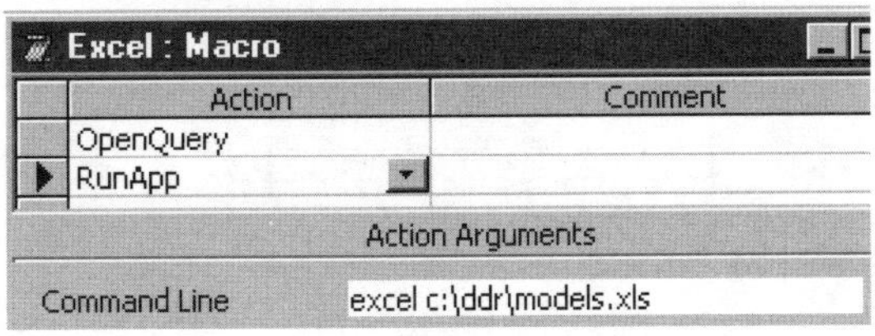

Figure 4.7. Defining actions.

4.5.3 Identification of a Type of Promotion for Further Analysis

The design of this form, depicting declining sales, is particularly useful in that the user can now select a particular promotion type for further analysis using the modelling environment. The promotion-type column in the form has an action-driven feature built into it. The user double clicks on any selected promotion type of interest. Such an action takes the interaction into the spreadsheet environment where the particular retailer, product and promotion-type combination is used for applying the models presented earlier.

Navigation from the database environment to the spreadsheet is achieved through the definition of actions to be taken when certain events occur in the database environment. An example of such an event is when a user double clicks on a particular promotion type in the form for further inspection. The actions that get triggered when this event occurs are:

1. The creation of a temporary table that contains all the data from the database necessary for modelling purposes; and
2. Opens up a spreadsheet in preparation for modelling aspects of the application.

Such a definition is attached to the form so that not only is the form useful in its own right, in terms of the data it displays, but also serves as a launching pad into the spreadsheet when such action is initiated by the user. Figure 4.7 below show how such definitions are constructed.

4.5.4 Optimal Spending for the Promotion

The spreadsheet environment is dynamically linked to a temporary table containing data that is necessary as input for the models discussed earlier. The temporary table is populated by the particular choice of retailer, product and promotion type by the user from the sales-decline form in the Access environment. The models are defined as

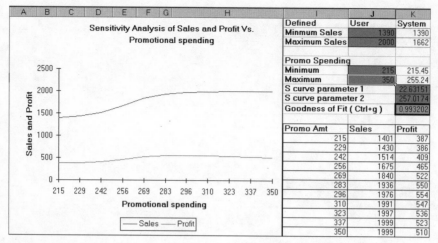

Figure 4.8. Modelling results.

expressions in the spreadsheet and applied to the data that is read from the database environment. At this point, default values for the model parameters are used to generate a graph showing the sales (profit) response to different levels of promotion spending as per the model specification. The user may interactively adjust parameter values directly on the spreadsheet in order to see its effects on the response characteristics. Repeated analysis using different combinations of retailer, product and promotion type may be conducted by seamlessly going from one environment to another. Figure 4.8 shows the display in the spreadsheet environment in the case of the ADBUDG model. Modelling with the MOBIL model is done using the same design principles.

4.5.5 Design Issues from the Spreadsheet Perspective

The link between the spreadsheet and database environments must be specifically established in such a way that the data required for modelling purposes are always available from the database in its current form. Several steps are involved in defining such a link. In this section we briefly describe how these steps are defined.

4.5.5.1 Definition of the Link from the Spreadsheet to the Database

After opening a new spreadsheet, provisions are made for obtaining the data required for modelling. This is accomplished by obtaining the data from a table containing the relevant data (the 'SalesPromoAmt' table defined in the Access database) through an Open Data Base Connectivity (ODBC) link. The ODBC link is setup through a sequence of steps as illustrated below:

1. In the spreadsheet go through the menu sequence Data $->$ Get External Data $->$ Create New Query, which results in the form shown below in Figure 4.9.
2. Set up a new data link by selecting < New Data Source > in the form above. This in turn results in the 'Create New Data Source' form shown in Figure 4.10 where the following are specified: the data link/source name, the driver type (in our case it is Microsoft Access Driver), the Access database name (PETAPS), and finally the name of the table in the database (SalesPromoAmt). This is shown in Figure 4.10.

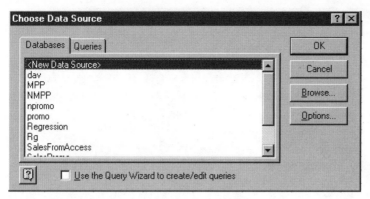

Figure 4.9. Linking the spreadsheet to the data – Step 1.

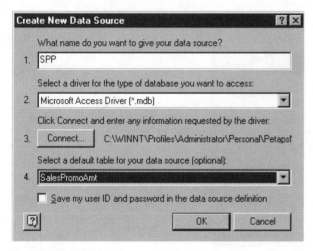

Figure 4.10. Linking the spreadsheet to the data – Step 2.

3. After setting up the data link specify what subset (horizontal and/or vertical) of the table are going to be accessed. This is done through the form shown in Figure 4.11.
4. Specify a spreadsheet location where the data will be placed as shown in the form in Figure 4.12.
5. Finally specify the properties of the link through the form shown in Figure 4.13. A couple of important properties that need to be set are the enabling of background refresh and the refreshment of data whenever the spreadsheet is opened. Once these properties have been set we can start modelling and/or manipulating the linked data.

4.5.5.2 Modelling with the Spreadsheet

The *maximum* and the *minimum sales* are suggested by PETAPS, based on historical data for the selected product–retailer–promotion-type combination as shown in Figure 4.8. The user can now either use the system suggestion or change the figures based on experience and knowledge. Similarly the *promotion spending range* (minimum and maximum) based on history is also suggested by the prototype which could be modified by the user. The *S-curve parameters* portray the market patterns. The application uses the *Solver* facility of *Excel* to calculate the *S-curve parameters* so that the *goodness of fit* to the historical data is

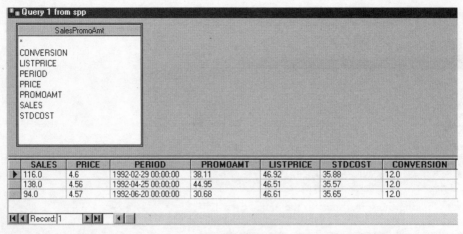

Query 1 from spp

SalesPromoAmt

CONVERSION
LISTPRICE
PERIOD
PRICE
PROMOAMT
SALES
STDCOST

SALES	PRICE	PERIOD	PROMOAMT	LISTPRICE	STDCOST	CONVERSION
116.0	4.6	1992-02-29 00:00:00	38.11	46.92	35.88	12.0
138.0	4.56	1992-04-25 00:00:00	44.95	46.51	35.57	12.0
94.0	4.57	1992-06-20 00:00:00	30.68	46.61	35.65	12.0

Record: 1

Figure 4.11. Linking the spreadsheet to the data: Step 3.

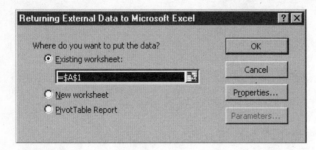

Figure 4.12. Linking the spreadsheet to the data: Step 4.

External Data Range Properties ? X

Name: ExternalData1

Query definition
☑ Save query definition
☑ Save password

Refresh control
☑ Enable background refresh
☑ Refresh data on file open
☐ Remove external data from worksheet before saving

Data layout
☐ Include field names   ☑ Autoformat data
☐ Include row numbers   ☑ Import HTML table(s) only

If the number of rows in the data range changes upon refresh:
⦿ Insert cells for new data, delete unused cells
○ Insert entire rows for new data, clear unused cells
○ Overwrite existing cells with new data, clear unused cells

☐ Fill down formulas in columns adjacent to data

OK   Cancel

Figure 4.13. Linking the spreadsheet to the data: Step 5.

best. The user can also input specific values for the *S-curve parameters* if that is appropriate.

Based on the user definition of minimum and maximum promotion amounts the system creates a series of promotion amounts that lie between the extremes. For each of these promotion amounts the sales value is predicted by the ADBUDG model (described earlier) using the parameter values (minimum sales, maximum sales, S-curve parameters). Apart from calculating the sales value we also calculate the profit for each of the sales figures using the formula shown below:

$$\text{Profit} = ((\text{List price} - \text{Standard cost})/\text{Conversion})^*\text{Sales} - \text{Promotion amount}$$

The sales and profit values obtained from the ADBUDG and profit models are graphed against the respective promotional spending values. Based on the above graphs, the user can arrive at the level of promotional spending that optimises sales and/or profit.

4.6 Lessons Learnt

We relate the approach to designing this system to the guiding architectural framework presented in Chapter 3. Figure 4.14 casts this framework in the specific context of the application under discussion. The organisation context is the manufacturing and marketing firm working on the problem of promotion of products in specific retail outlets. The problem has both data and model aspects that need to be presented to a marketing manager. The implementation relied on Access and Excel to serve these needs with the interaction being facilitated by the capabilities that are built into those two environments. The implementation used a modular design where the 'best-of-breed' software (specialist capabilities) was used to deliver parts of the solution that were finally integrated using ODBC connectivity.

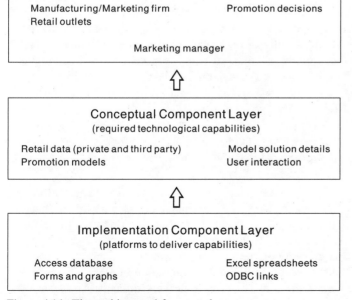

Figure 4.14. The architectural framework.

PETAPS supports the user in making informed promotion decisions. The decisions are based on historical data and market trends. The decision to select a product and retailer for a promotion is based on the decline in cash sales or volume of products sold. The selection of the type of promotion is based on historical data, analysis of past promotions and the current market conditions. Determination of optimal promotional spending is based on marketing models proven to be useful in similar consumer-goods industries. An important component of model building is the assessment of a model's ability to replicate a known data set. In PETAPS a facility was provided by which the models could be fine-tuned to reflect the market conditions specific to a product–retailer-type of promotion combination using the goodness-of-fit index. PETAPS enables the user to develop a better conceptualisation of the marketing environment and the role played by the promotions. The user's understanding of the effects of marketing variables, such as price and promotions on sales and profits, can be enhanced by the use of this DSS.

There are several aspects about DSS-type systems that were incorporated in this implementation. These systems are interactive and try to integrate diverse data and models to provide flexible support to managers and decision makers. Their usefulness is particularly great in areas of decision making where the problems tend to be relatively open ended and less well structured. They are designed to help the manager in modelling the decision process and provide a flexible and user-friendly interface that assists in carrying out sensitivity and other kinds of analyses with ease. It has been suggested that one of the key benefits of using a DSS is that it enables the manager to understand the business better and sharpen their intuition. While the concept of DSS has matured over recent years, the emergence of powerful workstations and a variety of sophisticated software tools have greatly facilitated the prototyping and implementation of systems that match this description.

Mini-Case: Ocean Spray Cranberries – Automated News Finding in Marketing

This mini-case is an excellent example of building a decision-support system for an organisational context that involves a large amount of data that will be manipulated by specific decision models. The results of data manipulation are presented to the user in a familiar and understandable format. In many respects, this is an example that is quite similar to the one discussed in Chapter 4. The reader should ask the appropriate design questions with respect to this application by thinking about the framework from Figure 3.1.

[Source: Schmitz, J. D., Armstrong, G. D. Little, J. D. C. (1990) CoverStory – Automated news finding in marketing, *Interfaces*, **20**(6).]

Ocean Spray Cranberries Inc. in 1990 was a billion-dollar grower-owned agricultural co-operative that produced and distributed juices and juice drinks with an emphasis on cranberry-based products. The database related with juices alone was huge: 400 million numbers, 100 data measures, 10,000 products, 125 weeks and 50 geographic markets. This database was growing at the rate of 10 million new numbers every week making the task of finding important trends or news amongst the detail and communicating it to the right people at the right time very difficult. The level of detail tended to obscure important trends and facts leading to the comment: 'We found that the news drowned in the detail.'

CoverStory – a decision support system – was developed by Information Resources Inc. (IRI) in partnership with Ocean Spray to specifically solve the problem of 'too much data'. Schmitz *et al.* (1990) report: 'CoverStory automates the creation of summary memoranda for reports extracted from large scanner databases. The goal is to provide a cover memo, like the one a marketing analyst would write, to describe key events that are reflected in the database – especially in its newest numbers ... CoverStory is very much a decision-support system rather than a decision-making system. The user can adjust all major system parameters, such as who competes with whom, what weights to use for the marketing factors, and how much information is to be reported.'

The DSS hardware architecture encompasses an IBM 9370 mainframe with 10 gigabytes of disk storage acting as the server and 11 client personal computers located in marketing and sales. The DSS software architecture includes at its core the IRI's DataServer, which uses the EXPRESS fourth-generation language to manage and manipulate data. pcEXPRESS – a user interface at the client workstations – makes it possible for menu-driven access to preprogrammed yet flexible reports. The open nature of the DSS architecture allows applications like CoverStory to be accessed from client workstations with ease.

The application had soon become an integral part of the operation of marketing management. It allowed managers to examine the impact of marketing strategies on product sales and monitor performance of various products vis-à-vis the competition. The delivery of the information to marketing professionals contributed to the success of the system: they received the information in a familiar memorandum format and were thus able to relate to it. According to the authors: 'the DSS has made it possible for a single marketing professional to manage the process of alerting all Ocean Spray marketing and sales managers to key problems and opportunities and to provide them with daily problem-solving information and guidance ... across four business units handling scores of company products in dozens of markets representing hundreds of millions of dollars of sales.'

References

Blattberg, R. C. and Wisniewski, K. J. (1986) Price-deduced patterns of competition, Working Paper, Graduate School of Business, University of Chicago.

Fotheringham, A. S. and Knudsen, D. C. (1987) *Concepts and Techniques in Modern Geography No. 46 – Goodness-of-fit Statistics*, Geo Books, Norwich, UK.

Islei, G., Lockett, G. Cox, B., Gisbourne, S. and Stratford, M. (1991) Modelling strategic decision making and performance measurements at ICI Pharmaceuticals, *Interfaces*, **21**(6), 4–22.

Keen, P. G. W. (1981) Value analysis: Justifying decision support systems, *MIS Quarterly*, **5**(1), 1–15.

Keen, P. G. W. and Morton, M. S. S. (1978) *Decision Support Systems: An Organisational Perspective*, Addison-Wesley Series on Decision Support, Addison-Wesley Publishing Company, Reading, Massachusetts, USA.

Lilien, G. L. (1986) *Marketing Mix Analysis with LOTUS 1-2-3*, The Scientific Press, Redwood City, California.

Little, J. D. C. (1975a) BRANDAID: A marketing-mix model, Part 1: Structure, *Operations Research*, **23**(4), 628–655.

Little, J. D. C. (1975b) BRANDAID: A marketing-mix model, Part 2: Implementation, Calibration, and Case Study, *Operations Research*, **23**(4), 656–673.

Little, J. D. C. (1979) Decision support systems for marketing managers, *Journal of Marketing*, **43**, 9–26.

Little, J. D. C. and Lodish, L. M. (1969) A media planning calculus, *Operations Research*, **17**(1), 1–35.

Naylor, T. H. and Shauland, H. (1976) A survey of users of corporate planning models, *Management Science*, **22**(9), 927–937.

Rao, A. G. and Lilien, G. L. (1972) A system of promotional models, *Management Science*, **19**(2), 152–160.

Sprague, R. H., Jr and Carlson, E. D. (1982) *Building Effective Decision Support Systems*, Englewood Cliffs, NJ: Prentice-Hall.

Wagner, G. R. (1979) Enhancing creativity in strategic planning through computer systems, *Managerial Planning*, **28**, 10–17.

DISCUSSION QUESTIONS

1. Using the 'best-of-breed' approach to building a DSS (several software packages each representing a design strength), describe an implementation architecture that harnesses the strengths of the different technologies while minimising the weaknesses.

2. Discuss the pros and cons of implementing DSS using a single integrated software platform (as opposed to multiple platforms chosen because of their unique strengths).

3. Critically evaluate PETAPS with respect to features that you expect in a flexible and visually interactive DSS.

4. Describe in detail the kind of system that you might build to support similar decisions as those supported by PETAPS. Your proposed system should take into account current technology, flexibility, visual interaction and design feasiblity.

5. Consider a decision-making situation of your choice. Focus on the modelling aspects of this situation and consider how you would support those aspects. Where would the data inputs for the models come from? How would you specify when a model should be used?

5

Object-Relational Database Systems

5.1 Introduction

In this chapter we highlight the usefulness of object-relational thinking and implementation. A major requirement of decision support applications is that we need to integrate data and modelling elements of a problem in a unified framework without curtailing the importance of either one. In Chapter 4 we saw one approach for dealing with this dual aspect of such applications. That approach involved working in two separate software environments by establishing explicit links between them. The alternative proposed in this chapter is to work within a single environment that offers features to deal with both aspects of problem solving. Object-oriented modelling is useful because it explicitly allows us to represent structural as well as behavioural aspects of a problem. This allows us to capture data and modelling components of our applications respectively. Further, by doing so within a single environment, we are able to leverage the advantages of modularity of design without sacrificing the ability to maintain the application in a straightforward manner. Finally, the best design is of little value if it cannot provide a convenient manner by which users may access the data contained in the application. By merging the advantages of relational systems with object-oriented concepts, object-relational database systems, (OR-DBMS) offer a full range of desirable capabilities for building decision support applications.

Computer-based support of complex decision-making problems requires the interaction of several diverse objects which can jointly capture accurate descriptions of the underlying problems. Specifically, we should consider rich representation schemes to capture the full extent of problem complexities. Such an idea refers not only to static notions of problem descriptions (snapshot representations of problems at particular points in time), but also encompasses dynamic aspects of an environment to reflect events and their consequent impact on data. Further, any useful decision-making support can only be facilitated by the ability of a system to represent varying degrees of complexity. This means that realistic problems involve individual items of data, combinations of such data in meaningful ways to reflect the structure of specific problems (models), and rules of manipulation whereby new data-item values are created as per specified rules of computation (solving algorithms). For example, consider an application where we want to keep track of the following data: production plants and their capacities, customers and their requirements, and the cost of transporting products from plants to customers. Specific relationships define the problem: products are shipped to customers to satisfy their demands subject to the production capacities of the plants. Such relationships should be captured in the application and we refer to these aspects as the modelling part of the application. Additionally, we may want to incorporate a data-manipulation rule that determines how much of a product to ship from each plant to each customer to satisfy demand so that the overall transportation cost is kept to a minimum value. The rule itself may be defined as part of the application and the specific manipulation of the data (regarding plants and customers), to determine the transported quantities and the total cost, can be invoked on demand by the user. Such a computation rule, which can be referenced by the application on demand, is referred to as a solver. It is a defined method for computing a result and is called a computation algorithm.

Modelling should be viewed as a process that involves a series of phases. The term 'life cycle' has been used to highlight the importance of this activity. Dealing with a problem that requires a model-based solution consists of initial problem definition and refinement, creating and/or invoking one or more accurate and formal model representations, appropriate linking of multiple models to accurately represent the problem at hand, ad hoc evaluation of the representation and maintenance of the representation over time. A modelling environment should support as much of this life cycle as possible.

Implementation platforms should recognise the importance of maintenance of a collection of models that may be called upon as needed. Modularity and independence are two design concepts that merit particular attention. A given problem may be completely novel in that it has to be described from scratch. This would be the case if we were dealing with the previously described transportation problem for the first time. Alternatively, it may be a new instance of a previously recognised problem (a new dataset). For instance, we may want to input new transportation-cost data and evaluate the task under the new cost scenario. Modular representation allows all variants of a particular problem to be supported. Sometimes, we may want to use multiple models and associated data to consider a single task. For example, customer demands may be determined by sales forecasts which gives rise to a forecasting module (with its associated model) and the transportation module. Maintenance is facilitated by ensuring that all modules of a system can be independently developed and edited, whether they are representation schemas, datasets or solving procedures. Finally, the access language must allow for a whole range of operations to be performed in a uniform and consistent manner. All these requirements can be implemented within an object-relational framework. In the next section we outline what such a framework entails and how database systems built on such a framework suit these requirements.

5.2 Object Relational Systems

Perhaps the best approach to understand the potential of OR-DBMS is to start with a list of functionalities that they offer. This will help us understand how they can be brought to bear on design problems of the type that we are interested in. A full fledged OR-DBMS provides traditional (relational) DBMS capabilities, incorporates object-oriented features that are seamlessly coupled with the DBMS features, and offers some functionality that is found neither in pure relational or object-oriented systems.[1]

Traditional functionality from relational systems that can be expected to be found in an OR-DBMS include:

- flexible data access through a standard Structured Query Language (SQL): this is the basic requirement of any database system that involves the ability of a user to conveniently access the contents of a database using a convenient query language;
- security controls: this provides for certain parts of the database to be selectively accessed by authorised users;

---

[1] An elaborate discussion of 'pure object oriented systems' is beyond the scope of this book. Section 5.3 provides a brief discussion of some important aspects of object orientation.

- server-enforced data integrity: this ensures that the data that is entered into the application is accurate and consistent;
- transaction management and recovery: this provides for the system to revert back to a correct state in the event of database failure;
- performance and scalability: this provides quick access to data which becomes an increasingly important issue as the size of the application gets larger.

Key object-oriented features that one may expect to find in an OR-DBMS include:

- open architecture/extensibility – not limited to the predefined built-in data types, and a system that could be tailored and extended to suit user requirements. To continue our example about the problem of transporting products to customers, it would be convenient to describe a *data type* called 'transportation link' that makes reference to a particular customer–plant combination with all the associated details. Such a data type is relevant in the particular context of the application and is therefore thought of as a 'user defined data type';
- facility to create user-defined functions/methods to act on the user-defined/abstract data types as well as existing/built-in data types. The computation rule for calculating the least-cost transportation plan can be defined as part of the definition of our task. Further the manipulation rule may be attached to selected data in the application to which the rule applies;
- single and multiple inheritance of both structure and behaviour with the option for late binding: we may wish to distinguish between production plants and distribution plants, both of which may serve customers. Inheritance allows us to recognise that these are both sources for customers but are different from each other in certain characteristics. Now a manipulation rule that refers to the movement of products from a plant may be interpreted differently depending on which particular type of plant applies in the particular situation.

Finally, one can expect OR-DBMS systems to possess features that neither relational nor object-oriented systems (in their traditional forms) exhibit such as:

- functions/methods that span types;
- extensions to the industry-standard familiar SQL to support objects.

Thus in some ways OR-DBMS attempt to have the best of both worlds. This is reflected in Stonebraker's (1996) classification of DBMS applications illustrated in Figure 5.1. The figure highlights the two major requirements of decision support applications: the need for supporting complex data and the ability of users to access the data through a convenient querying interface. It shows that relational systems have a query-language requirement that is not typically shared by object-oriented systems; and object-oriented systems can deal with complex data that relational systems cannot handle. Hence the benefits of merging these two capabilities in a manner that retains the best of both worlds should be obvious.

	Simple data	Complex data
Query	Relational DBMS	Object-relational DBMS
No query	File system	Object-oriented DBMS

Figure 5.1. Classification of DBMS applications (from Stonebraker, 1996).

Another useful way in which to think about object-relational systems is proposed by Kim (1996) in a manner that formalises some of the ideas discussed previously. He describes object oriented and other extensions to the relational model that results in the object-relational data model. (Although we have discussed key features of relational systems in Chapter 3, we reiterate those points that are central to the discussion in this chapter.) Some relevant aspects of the relational model are first discussed to show how the extensions provided by object-relational models fit into this conceptualisation.

The relational database consists of a set of relations (types). A relation consists of rows (instance of a type) and columns (attributes). A column entry in a row of a relation can have a *single value* that belongs to a set of system-defined data types (integer, float, string, date, boolean, etc.). There are four key extensions to the relational data model that results in the object-relational model:

1. Acceptable values under a specific column of a relation can be a row of any arbitrary user-defined relation, rather than being restricted to a single value of a system-defined data type. This implies that the user can specify an arbitrary user-defined relation as the domain of a relation. This leads to nested relations where the value of a row/column entry of a relation can now be a row of another relation. Hence a column entitled 'plant' to contain data about product sources for customers might contain a row of data with all details about a plant instead of just an identification of a particular plant.

2. The row/column entry of a relation can have a set of values of any data type – system defined or user defined. This is in contrast to the relational model which allows each row/column entry to have only one value. This reduces the duplication of data as well the creation of structures that are semantically more meaningful than traditional data models. For example, a column entitled 'demand' to store product-demand data for a customer may contain a set of demand data that shows the demand for a set of products. This way we are able to refer to the entire set of demand values using a single column or attribute.

3. Procedures/methods can be attached to relations and the procedures can operate on the column values in each row. Thus the relation encapsulates the state and behaviour of its rows. We can thus define a procedure that calculates the cost of transporting products to a customer by attaching it to the customer relation.

4. Relations can be organised into a hierarchy such that type and subtype relationships may be expressed in a straightforward manner. As pointed out in a previous example, this allows us to express different types of plants as different classes but yet retain their similarities since they both act as sources for customers.

Though these extensions may appear minor, the collective impact on the ease of modelling complex domains is significant. In the following paragraphs we elaborate on some concepts and the functionality offered by OR-DBMS. Readers familiar with object-oriented systems will see the incorporation of those concepts into OR-DBMSs.

5.3 Key Modelling Elements

5.3.1 Data Types

There are two categories of data types:

- data types packaged with the system such as built-in types and system types;

- user-defined data types that a user can create such as base types, composite types and constructed types.

Data types packaged with the system are:

- built-in types like integer, floating-point, character, date/time, boolean, etc.;
- system types like object identifiers (oid) and other types used for system administration.

Data types that a user can build or define are:

- base types – fundamental atomic types that require the user to define input and output functions for conversion from external representation to internal representation and vice versa;
- constructed types – for any type registered/available in the system whether built in or user defined the system supports an array of that type (e.g. arrayof(integer), arrayof(text)), a set of that type (e.g. setof(employee_t), setof(person_t)) and a reference to objects of that type (e.g. ref(employee_t), ref(person_t));
- composite types – grouping of already-existing typed components, these components could be base (e.g. integer, real, text), constructed (e.g. setof(employee_t), ref(employee_t), etc.) or composite (e.g. employee_t, person_t, address_t). It provides storage for complex data that consists of multiple members.

5.3.2 Methods/Functions that Operate on Data Types

There are two categories of functions:

- Built-in functions that operate on the data types that come packaged with the system. Examples of built-in functions are arithmetic functions, text functions, comparative functions, date/time functions, aggregates (average, count, max, min and sum), etc.
- User-defined functions that can operate on not only user-defined types but also on the types that the system comes packaged with. The user-defined function could be created using just SQL or, if the function is complex, a procedural language like C or C++ or Stored Procedure Language (SPL) can be used to create the function. Apart from this, the user can also define aggregate functions over the user-defined types or new types of aggregation over system-defined types.

5.3.3 Containment Hierarchies

The composite user-defined type could be used to build containment hierarchies. This is similar to the concept of hierarchies of aggregation abstractions (Smith and Smith 1977). In the pure relational model, it is difficult to understand how a collection of relations is actually modelling a system. Transformation of a relationship between several objects into a higher level object, also known as aggregation, helps to increase the understandability of a model. This kind of aggregation abstraction can be naturally implemented using the composite user-defined type to build containment hierarchies.

5.3.4 Type Hierarchies

The inheritance mechanism allows us to build a hierarchy of types of objects. This is similar to the concept of hierarchies of generalisation abstractions (Smith and Smith 1977), where a set of similar objects is regarded as a generic object. Inheritance or generalisation is also sometimes called subtyping or subclassing. A few definitions to help understand the mechanism of inheritance are explained below:

> *Type B is said to be a subtype of type A – equivalently type A is said to be a supertype of B – if every object of type B is also an object of type A. Then objects of type B inherit the structure (structural inheritance) and methods (behavioural inheritance) that apply to type A. This implies that methods that apply on objects of type A can also apply on objects of type B – that is, because of inheritance we are able to apply different methods with the same name to different types. This kind of polymorphism is known as inheritance polymorphism.*

5.3.5 Access Languages

Object-relational DBMS retain most of the features of the industry standard SQL and include features that provide object-oriented functionality. They are compatible with the proposed ANSI standard for SQL3. This extended SQL (ESQL) supports object-oriented features such as abstract data types, user-defined functions and inheritance while remaining compatible with previous versions of SQL. Thus the interface is familiar to many decision makers, modellers and programmers. The user defined and system-defined functions act as natural extensions to the SQL language. Apart from ESQL most OR-DBMS also offer graphical user interfaces and embedded ESQL in a procedural language. These could be used to manipulate models, data and solvers.

5.4 Task-driven Rationale

Having discussed the object-relational features that are useful to designing decision support applications, we now focus on the typical tasks that are encountered during the design process and map them to object-relational capabilities. Table 5.1 shows a typical task typology in a decision support environment. It also shows the linkages between elements of this task typology and the object-relational environment. Four classes of tasks

Table 5.1. Linkages between tasks and object-relational environment.

Task	Object-relational implications
Class 1: Declaration (specification) of: • data • models • solvers	• Abstract data typing that allows for representing objects of arbitrary complexity. • Ability to specify functions declaratively. • Ability to link to procedural-language specifications for solver implementation.
Class 2: Instantiation of base objects	• Access language enables user-initiated object instantiation. • Function specification enables even-triggered instantiation.
Class 3: Integration of: • models and data • models and solvers • models and models	• Function parameters and returned values are attributes belonging to declared objects. • The combination of procedural and declarative functions allow flexible integration of models and solvers. • Rule system allows model linkage.

are defined. The first class is the initial specification of objects in the application. These objects may be related to data elements. Alternatively, they may be related to simple or complex computational rules acknowledged at a more abstract level by models and at the implementation level by solvers. The abstract data-typing capability of the object-relational framework allows the representation of objects. Furthermore, functions may be specified declaratively. More complex manipulations, as in the case of specialised solvers, may be handled by the links to procedural languages.

The second class of tasks refers to the instantiation of represented objects. The user interface of the object-relational system plays a crucial role here. The language interfaces available are based on the time-tested principles of associative query languages which have a long history of success in the database-management domain and shows ample promise for this approach. Instantiation may also be event triggered as opposed to being explicitly initiated by the user. In such cases, event-triggered instantiation of objects is a capability that proves to be useful.

The third class of tasks involves the integration of various types of objects in an application. The simplest type of integration is the combining of data with models to explore solutions. Furthermore, these functions may be explicitly specified in multiple ways in the object-relational environment. Another type of integration involves the combining of models with solvers. The implication of this type of integration is that there might be multiple solution methods (e.g. two different optimisation algorithms) to implement a given model solution. By maintaining independence between models and solvers, such linking is provided by object-relational systems in a straightforward manner using the access language. Finally, two models might need combining in a given circumstance (e.g. a forecasting model might provide the output that indicates the demand for a product, which is the input in a distribution model). The rule system of the object-relational environment enables the implementation of such integration.

5.4.1 Implementation

In this section we explore how the implementation ideas outlined in Table 5.1 may be executed in an OR-DBMS environment. The specific platform used for this is the Informix OR-DBMS. We do this by taking two specific problems and dealing with representation and manipulation issues as per a set of representative tasks. In doing this, we seek to highlight (a) the distinctions between data, models and solvers and the modularity and independence carried through in their construction, (b) the uniformity of expression regardless of whether the task is data retrieval or function invocation (i.e. data transformation based on solvers), and (c) integration of multiple model representations.

5.4.2 The Satellite Problem (Geoffrion, 1992)

A satellite in orbit around the Earth can be pulled away from its path by other objects that pass close to it. Therefore it is crucial to find out what kinds of objects at what distances pose a threat to the satellite. If the force of attraction between the satellite and object exceeds 10^{-6} newton, then the satellite gets pulled into a dysfunctional orbit. The factors that are of importance in calculating whether an object is a threat to the satellite or not are: the mass of the object, the mass of the satellite, and the distance between the object and the satellite. Furthermore, the mass of an object and its distance might be drawn from a distribution suggesting the need for incorporating such uncertainty in the specification

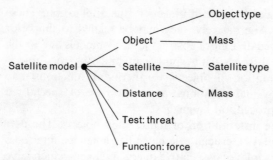

Figure 5.2. Modular structure of the satellite model.

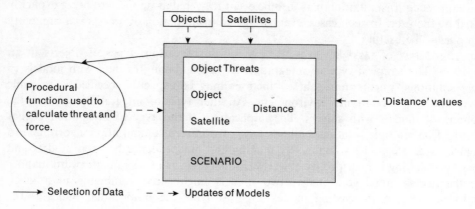

Figure 5.3. The satellite problem – dynamic aspects.

and evaluation of force and threat. Newton's law of gravitation gives the force between the object and the satellite:

$$\text{Force} = (6.67 \times 10^{-11} \times \text{Satellite mass}$$

$$\times (\text{Object mass}) / \text{Distance between the satellite and object})^2$$

From an implementation perspective the essential components of the problem involve (a) datasets reflecting the existence of various satellites and objects; (b) a function that performs a force computation (and others that are consequences of force) based on the specified law; and (c) the construction of problem instances defining chosen satellite–object pairs (scenarios). The problem in modular outline for the satellite model is shown in Figure 5.2.

We now proceed to demonstrate (a) data and model instantiation and retrieval, and (b) function specification and utilisation by a series of implementation session scripts. The access language is a modification of SQL to incorporate abstract data typing and function specification. Figure 5.3 is a depiction of the dynamic aspects of the problem to highlight flows of data and the impact of function invocation.

5.4.3 Examples

5.4.3.1 Definition of Classes and the Associated Data

We first create the *satellite* and *object* classes by defining the data types involved. Note that, as part of this exercise, we introduce both satellite and object as data types as well, allowing us to refer to instances of these types if necessary.

creation of satellite
```
create row type satellite_t (satellite varchar(10), mass
                                           decimal(2));
create table satellite of type satellite_t;
```

creation of object
```
create row type object_t (object varchar(10), mass decimal(2));
create table object of type object_t;
```

We are now ready to insert data regarding satellites and objects of interest in our application into the appropriate tables just defined.

Insertion of satellites
```
insert into satellite values ('Telstar1',500);
insert into satellite values ('SpareSat',200);
```

Insertion of objects
```
insert into object values('Comet X',10000);
insert into object values('Comet 3B',20000);
insert into object values('Spacecom',5000);
```

The contents of the satellite and object relations can now be viewed using traditional SQL type statements.

Eliciting details
```
select * from satellite;
```

	satellite	mass
1	Telstar1	500
2	SpareSat	200

```
select * from object;
```

	object	mass
1	Comet X	10000
2	Comet 3B	20000
3	Spacecom	5000

5.4.3.2 Definition and Use of Functions

As noted in the discussion of the problem, objects pose specific threats to satellites based on the distance between them. The assessment of the threat posed by a specific object to a specific satellite with a specified distance between them can be dealt with in a variety of ways. We can evaluate the threat based on the expression for force from Section 5.4.2 by embedding the computation as part of the statement itself. This is shown below. The example compares the threat between every satellite–object pair in the application when we consider a distance of 10 between them and produces a column called 'threat' which contains a boolean value ('true' or 'false'). A value of 't' indicates that the given pair constitutes a threat (under the circumstances) while a value of 'f' indicates the absence of a threat. Hence, simple functions can be directly captured in the construction of the query.

```
select s.satellite,s.mass, o.object, o.mass,
((((0.0000000000667*s.mass*o.mass)/(10*10))>0.000001) threat
from object o, satellite s;
```

	satellite	mass	object	mass	threat
1	Telstar1	500	Comet X	10000	t
2	Telstar	500	Comet 3B	20000	t
3	Telstar1	500	Spacecom	5000	t
4	SpareSat	200	Comet X	10000	t
5	SpareSat	200	Comet 3B	20000	t
6	SpareSat	200	Spacecom	5000	f

An alternative manner by which such functions may be defined and maintained as part of the application is shown below. This offers the user a great deal of flexibility in the use of function that is defined by the user and is an integral part of the application. Here the function *threat* is defined procedurally (using the language feature SPL that is part of the Informix platform) to show the inputs and the output. Once the definition is accepted by the system, it is available for use as part of a traditional query, as shown in the example below.

```
Definition of the function
CREATE FUNCTION threat (smass decimal, omass decimal, distance
                                                    integer)
RETURNING boolean;
define i boolean;
IF (((0.0000000000667*smass*omass)/(distance*distance))
                                                    >0.000001)
then
let i = 't';
  else
let i = 'f';
END IF
RETURN i;
END FUNCTION;
```

5.4.3.3 Use of the Function Within an SQL Statement Using a Distance Value of 15 metres

```
select s.satellite, o.object, threat (s.mass, o.mass, 15) threat
from object o, satellite s
order by threat desc, satellite, object;
```

	satellite	object	threat
1	SpareSat	Comet 3B	t
2	Telstar1	Comet 3B	t
3	Telstar1	Comet X	t
4	SpareSat	Comet X	f
5	SpareSat	Spacecom	f
6	Telstar1	Spacecom	f

To provide another example of defining and using functions, we consider the *force* function where the force between a satellite and an object is computed. The function is then used as part of a traditional SQL statement.

```
CREATE FUNCTION force (smass decimal, omass decimal, distance
                                                      integer)
RETURNING decimal;
define i decimal;
let i = ((0.0000000000667*smass*omass)/(distance*distance));
RETURN i;
END FUNCTION;
```

The following shows the execution of the *force* function within an SQL statement for a distance value of 15 metres. In the first case the actual value of force is displayed, while in the second case the threat posed by the particular force is evaluated and displayed.

```
select s.satellite, o.object, force( s.mass, o.mass, 15) force
from object o, satellite s
order by satellite, object;
```

	satellite	object	force
1	SpareSat	Comet 3B	1.18577777777778e-06
2	SpareSat	Comet X	5.92888888888889e-07
3	SpareSat	Spacecom	2.96444444444444e-07
4	Telstar1	Comet 3B	2.96444444444444e-06
5	Telstar1	Comet X	1.48222222222222e-06
6	Telstar1	Spacecom	7.41111111111111e-07

```
select s.satellite, o.object,
(force (s.mass, o.mass, 15) >0.000001) threat
from object o, satellite s
order by threat desc, satellite, object;
```

	satellite	object	threat
1	SpareSat	Comet 3B	t
2	Telstar1	Comet 3B	t
3	Telstar1	Comet X	t
4	SpareSat	Comet X	f
5	SpareSat	Spacecom	f
6	Telstar1	Spacecom	f

5.4.3.4 Introducing Distance

Finally, in order to consider a distribution of distance values for evaluating threats, we can use a distance table as shown below. There are alternative ways by which such a distribution may be generated. For example, it is possible to draw random values of distances from a random-number generator that is provided as a part of many DBMS.

```
select * from distance;
```

	distance
1	15
2	20
3	25
4	30
5	35
6	40
7	100

The data from the distance table can now be used in conjunction with the threat function described previously.

```
select s.satellite, o.object, d.distance, threat (s.mass,
                                   o.mass,d.distance) threat
from object o, satellite s, distance d
order by threat desc, satellite;
```

	satellite	object	distance	threat
1	SpareSat	Comet 3B	15	t
2	Telstar1	Comet 3B	25	t
3	Telstar	Comet 3B	20	t
4	Telstar1	Comet 3B	15	t
5	Telstar1	Comet X	15	t
6	SpareSat	Comet X	15	f
7	SpareSat	Spacecom	15	f
8	SpareSat	Comet 3B	25	f
9	SpareSat	Comet X	25	f
10	SpareSat	Comet X	20	f
11	SpareSat	Comet 3B	20	f
12	SpareSat	Spacecom	20	f
13	SpareSat	Spacecom	1000	f

In this section we have shown through simple examples some powerful capabilities that exist in OR-DBMS. It is particularly important to note that our ability to represent functions provides us with an essential requirement of many decision support applications. In the following section, we go on to another example where we can explore the modelling process and its implementation more fully using OR-DBMS platforms.

5.5 Supporting the Modelling Life-Cycle Rationale

The notion of a modelling life cycle was introduced in Chapter 2. To briefly summarise that discussion, the key phases in the life-cycle process are:

1. formulation of the model;
2. integration of the model with appropriate solvers;
3. integration of the model with data/instantiation of the model;
4. storage of the model;
5. retrieval of model-instance information;
6. use/execution of the model;
7. reformulation of the model if necessary;
8. termination or removal of the model;
9. integration of multiple models;
10. perform *what-if* analysis on the model by changing the solvers and/or data and/or model versions;
11. retrieval of information relating to the structure and behaviour of the model.

The object-relational approach enables us to support most of the modelling life cycle. In the examples below we highlight OR-DBMS support for some of the key modelling phases.

5.5.1 Product Sales Forecasting

Product sales forecasting is an activity that is conducted by numerous firms on a periodic basis. Because of the nature of the task it lends itself very well to the application of decision support tools. In the classic forecasting case we will have historical data regarding the sales of a number of products, which are then used to forecast the future sales of the products. The forecasted sales for the products could be accomplished using any one of a variety of solvers or algorithms such as: exponential smoothing, regression, moving average, etc. These are all alternative methods for generating forecasts. Through examples we demonstrate the flexibility of design that is offered in the application in terms of our ability to pick and choose among several available solvers. We use this simple but ubiquitous scenario to illustrate the decision modelling life-cycle support provided by the Informix OR-DBMS.

5.5.2 Object-Relational Representation of the Forecasting Schema – Model Formulation

The product forecasting model is implemented/represented through the creation of an abstract data type (ADT) *product_t* whose structure is shown in Figure 5.4. The attributes of the product that are relevant for this case are: *pcode*, *sales* and *forecast*. The ability to model complex data types allows us to represent sales histories and multiple forecasts with lists. The behaviour of the product forecasting model/ADT *product_t* is represented by functions *es* (exponential smoothing) and *regress* (regression) whose inputs are the sales of a product over a number of periods (a *LIST(integers)*). The output of the functions is a decimal value. Apart from these two base functions other functions will be defined to highlight specific features of using OR-DBMS that allow for complete modelling life-cycle support.

The creation of the model structure, behaviour and model-instance holding table are illustrated in the following paragraphs. In defining some of the functions, we utilise the

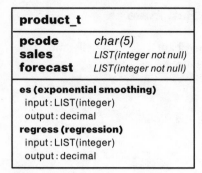

product_t	
pcode	*char(5)*
sales	*LIST(integer not null)*
forecast	*LIST(integer not null)*
es (exponential smoothing) input : LIST(integer) output : decimal **regress (regression)** input : LIST(integer) output : decimal	

Figure 5.4. Product sales forecasting model.

Stored Procedure Language (SPL) provided by the Informix environment. The procedural nature of the language (compared with SQL) provides a measure of flexibility in the definition of the functions. Clearly, any procedural language could be used for this purpose.

5.5.2.1 Creation of the Product Forecasting Model Structure

```
create row type product_t (   pcode     char(5),
                              sales     LIST(integer not null),
                              forecast  LIST(integer not null));
```

5.5.2.2 Creation of the Product Forecasting Model-instance Storage Table

```
create table product of type product_t;
```

5.5.2.3 Creation of the Product Forecasting Model Behaviour (functions defined using SPL)

Exponential Smoothing Function

```
CREATE     function es(thelist LIST(integer not null))
           returning decimal(8,1);
DEFINE alpha, forecast decimal;
DEFINE n,  theelement integer;
LET forecast=0;
LET alpha=0.7;
LET n=0;
FOREACH cursor1 FOR
    SELECT * INTO theelement FROM TABLE(thelist)
    IF n=0 THEN
        LET forecast = theelement;
        LET n=1;
    END IF;
    LET forecast=(alpha)*theelement+(1-alpha)*forecast;
    CONTINUE FOREACH;
END FOREACH
LET forecast=(alpha)*theelement+(1-alpha)*forecast;
RETURN forecast;
END function;
```

Regression Function

```
CREATE     function regress(thelist LIST(integer not null))
           returning decimal(8,1);
DEFINE forecast decimal(8,1);
DEFINE t,t1,t2,t3,t4,n, theelement integer;
DEFINE slope, intercept decimal;
LET t1 = 0;
LET t2 = 0;
LET t3 = 0;
LET t4 = 0;
LET t = 1;
LET n = cardinality(thelist);
FOREACH cursor1 FOR
     SELECT * INTO theelement FROM TABLE(thelist)
     LET t1 = t1+1;
     LET t2 = t2+ theelement;
     LET t3 = t3+(t*t);
     LET t4 = t4+t*theelement;
     LET t = t+1;
     CONTINUE FOREACH;
END FOREACH
LET slope = (n*t4 - t2*t1)/(n*t3-t1*t1);
LET intercept = (t2/n) - (slope)*(t1/n);
LET forecast = (intercept +(slope*(n+1)));
RETURN forecast;
END function;
```

5.5.3 Instantiation of the Model

The model storage table can be instantiated in a variety of ways. The example below shows the creation of a new product-forecasting model instance.

5.5.3.1 Insertion of a New Model Instance

```
insert into product
values('P1',
       "LIST{200,135,195,197, 310,175,155,130,220,277,235}",
       "LIST{}");
```

5.5.4 Elicitation of Model Instance Information

An example that elicits the forecasting model instance information and the result of such an elicitation is shown below. The statements elicit information at different levels of the model.

Model Instance Information

```
select * from product;
```

	pcode	sales	forecast
1	P1	list(11) of integer	list(1) of integer

The *sales* column indicates that it contains a list made up of 11 integers. Double clicking on the *sales* column will produce the following output:

1	200
2	135
3	195
4	197
5	310
6	175
7	155
8	130
9	220
10	277
11	235

5.5.5 Modification of the Model Instance

An important aspect of this environment is its ability to provide dynamic update of model-instance data through simple queries. We could update the values of any set of attributes in a particular model instance as illustrated in the following example.

5.5.5.1 Model-instance Update

```
update    product
          set sales =
          "LIST{220,135,195,197,310,175,155,130,220,277,235}"
          where pcode='P1';
```

Although this might look like a trivial example, it should be pointed out that instance update usually involves a complicated process of editing data files in traditional modelling environments. One of the advantages of the OR-DBMS environment is that such updates are handled in a consistent manner through the query interface.

5.5.6 Execution of the Model

Once all the data relevant to the problem are in the model-instance storage structure (table) we are ready to execute the functions that result in the execution of the model. The following example illustrates the use of the exponential smoothing function *es*.

5.5.6.1 Execution of 'es' to Forecast the Sale of Products in the Next Period

```
select pcode, es(sales) from product;
```

	pcode	forecast
1	P1	236.6

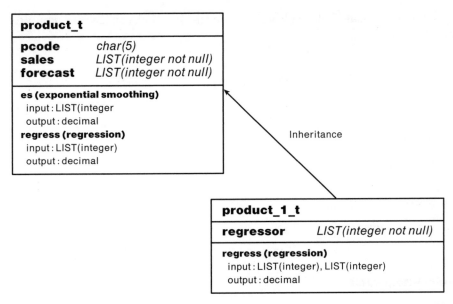

Figure 5.5. Using inheritance to modify model structure.

5.5.7 Modification of the Model

There are three ways in which we can modify or change a model: instance, structure or behaviour. Instance modification has already been dealt with in Section 5.5.5. Adding new parts to an existing model may be accomplished by using inheritance. This has the advantage of the original model structure being undisturbed and the new structure becoming a version of the original model structure. We illustrate this by creating a new version of the forecasting model. The new version and its relation to the original (Figure 5.4) is shown in Figure 5.5. One new attribute is declared in the newly derived model (ADT). The new attribute acts as an independent variable for a regression algorithm to forecast the sales of products. New functions or solvers may be similarly declared if necessary. The complete structure of *product_t* and all the functions that apply to *product_t* and its components are inherited by *product_1_t*. Adding and removing functions and solvers to enhance or curtail the range of behaviours is achieved in a straightforward manner via function-oriented maintenance-related statements.

5.5.8 Termination of the Model

Termination of a model could mean the removal/deletion of a model instance or the removal of the model itself with all the model storage structures, model behaviour and model structure. The deletion of a model instance is shown below:

5.5.8.1 Model-instance Deletion

```
delete from product where pcode='P1';
```

This statement deletes the model instance that meets the criteria of *pcode* being equal to *P1*. The removal of a complete model – that is, its structure and behaviour – is a bit more complex. We buy model-data independence and model-solver independence in return for this complexity.

5.5.8.2 *Model Storage Structure Deletion*

```
drop table product;
```

5.5.8.3 *Model Behaviour Deletion*

```
drop function es;
```

5.5.8.4 *Model Structure Deletion*

```
drop row type product_t restrict;
```

5.5.9 Model Integration

Model integration is a crucial phase in the modelling life cycle described earlier. There are many different ways by which models could be integrated. We might want to integrate results from executing the solver many times, once for each instance. In the following example we show a situation where we are aggregating several product forecasts obtained by using the exponential smoothing solver *es* to form a single family-level forecast.

5.5.9.1 *Aggregating the Results Obtained from the Multiple Executions of the 'es' Solver*

```
select sum(es(sales)) from product;
```

	(sum)
1	962.8

Another example of model integration is a situation where we might want to consolidate the execution results obtained from two different solvers. In the following example a weighted average of product forecasts is obtained by consolidating the outputs from the exponential smoothing and regression solvers.

5.5.9.2 *Consolidating the Results Obtained from the Execution of Two Different Solvers*

```
select  pcode,
        es(sales) as es,
        regress(sales) as regress,
        (es(sales)*0.60+regress(sales)*0.40) as consolidated
  from product;
```

	pcode	es	regress	consolidated
1	P1	236.6	463.9	327.52
2	P2	726.2	1193.0	912.92

A third type of integration is 'pipelining' where the results from one solver/model become input to another. The example of aggregation discussed earlier is in itself an example of pipelining where the results of *es* are sent to the summing function *sum*. The function *es* is nested within the summing function *sum*. This nesting of solvers/functions achieves the desired result.

The examples of integration seen above are of an ad hoc nature where integration is achieved on the fly. Alternatively, we might want a permanent integration of models or their parts in the construction of new and larger models. The example of model-structure modification from Section 5.5.7 shows the creation of a larger model by combining existing components with new ones.

5.5.10 Exploring Modelling Scenarios

In typical decision support applications we are interested in examining the effects of perturbations in the model. These perturbations could involve changes to data values, parameters, specific solvers that are used and/or specific models. The performance of a forecasting solver may be assessed in some circumstances by examining the impact of different parameter values on the forecasted results. The following example allows us to execute one function twice so that we could compare the results obtained with different values of the parameter.

5.5.10.1 Modelling Scenario: Case 1

```
select   escm(sales,.5) as alpha1,
         escm(sales,.9) as alpha2 from product;
```

	pcode	alpha1			alpha2		
		forecast	forecastlist	mape	forecast	forecastlist	mape
1	P1	233.9	list(11) of decimal	29.9323008269944	238.5	list(11) of decimal	32.1255500891507
2	P2	671.5	list(11) of decimal	19.6357544257277	727.7	list(11) of decimal	20.9221365911810

As a decision maker we might be interested in comparing the effects of two different forecasting methods (solvers) on the forecasted result. In the following example we use two different solvers to generate product forecasts. Specifically the solvers are exponential smoothing (*escm*) and regression (*reg*).

5.5.10.2 Modelling Scenario: Case 2

```
select    pcode,
          escm(sales,.9) as exponentialsmooth,
          reg(sales) as regression
        from product;
```

	pcode	exponentialsmooth			regression		
		forecast	forecastlist	mape	forecast	slope	intercept
1	P1	238.5	list(11) of decimal	32.1355500891507	463.9	23.5838383838384	180.870707070707
2	P2	727.7	list(11) of decimal	20.9221365911810	1193.0	63.5838383838384	429.961616161616

5.5.11 Elicitation of Model Information: Meta Data

Information regarding the model characteristics (meta data) can be elicited by querying the system catalogues using SQL. Apart from using SQL for eliciting information regarding model structure and behaviour we can also use *Schema Knowledge*, an add-on to the Informix OR-DBMS. *Schema Knowledge* allows us to see the model in the database in relation to other models, and also to view the detailed structure and behaviour of the models. *Schema Knowledge* enables access to meta-information about the system, but not actual data, and does not permit any changes to the model schema. It allows the modeller to explore the structure of the model at different levels of detail (Figures 5.6 and 5.7).

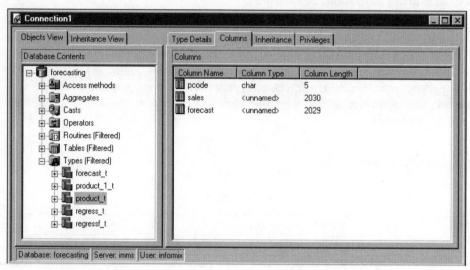

Figure 5.6. Elicit information regarding the structure of the forecasting model.

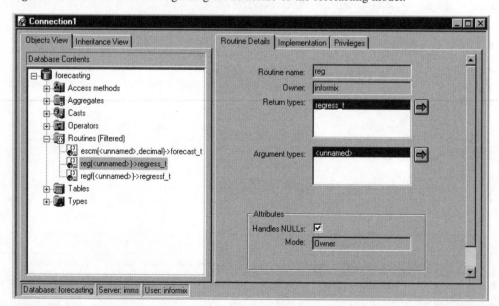

Figure 5.7. Elicit information regarding the behaviour of the forecasting model.

5.6 Conclusion

Figure 5.8 indicates how the two major applications discussed in this chapter relate to the overall architectural framework that we proposed in Chapter 3. The organisational contexts of the two applications are satellite monitoring and product management. Specifically, we wish to monitor the movements of satellites and objects in space in one case, and perform product sales forecasting in the other. The data implications have to do with satellite and object-related data such as mass and distance in the former application and product sales data in the other. Models for calculating force and collision threats are critical in the first application while various forecasting models and their integration are critical in the second. The implementation strategy employed a single object-relational platform that delivered all aspects of the conceptual capabilities under a single-software environment, thereby negating the need for integrating several independently developed modules.

Earlier, in Chapter 3, we introduced the concept of object-relational modelling and illustrated the ideas involved through some simple examples. In this chapter we follow up that introduction with some examples that more fully explore the functionality offered by this environment. The important point to reiterate is that object-relational systems allow us to design applications with complex data. Additionally, a key benefit is the ability of the designer to incorporate complex manipulations of the data as an integral part of the application. This allows us to specify both data and modelling aspects (important requirements for a decision support application) within a single-design environment. We provided a task-based rationale for the need for using such systems and showed, through examples, how the capabilities of these systems may be leveraged in the process of designing decision support systems. We also examined how such a system can provide support for many phases of the modelling life cycle. While the data aspects of a prototypical application are at least as important as its modelling aspects, we emphasise the interaction between them in the examples developed in this chapter.

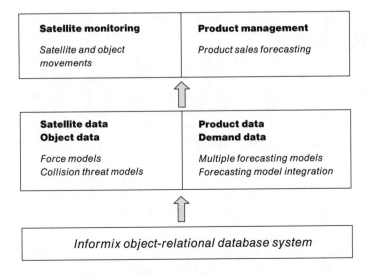

Figure 5.8. The architecture of the applications.

Mini-Case: First Union Corporation: Knowledge-based Marketing

This mini-case is an example where the organisational context presents a complex mixture of data, models and analysis to support the marketing function in a financial institution. The choice of an object-relational platform to implement this data-intensive application reflects the need to handle many aspects of complex data and couple that with the integration of third-party software tools for analysis.

[Source: That Personal Touch, *Informix Magazine*, **3**(2), Spring 1999.]

First Union Corporation is the sixth-largest banking company in the US with $237 billion in assets and 16 million customers, who provide an enormous amount of information through their transactions about their purchasing habits, locations they prefer, banking preferences, etc. To better utilise this data the company recently invested in a $27-million data warehousing and decision-support project which is expected to increase its revenue by $100 million annually. As Naras Eechambadi (Senior Vice-president of *Knowledge Based Marketing* at First Union) says, 'You can't make money unless you have good information, which you get from your data . . . Information flow precedes cash flow.'

First Union identified the need to build a system that would integrate all the customer data sources and would allow decision makers to access as well as perform dynamic time-series analysis and detect patterns about customer behaviour. The system at the heart of the solution is an enterprise data warehouse implemented using the Informix Dynamic Server with extended parallel and advanced decision-support options and running on an IBM RS/6000 with 250 processors. Initially populated with around 2 terabytes (factor of 10^{12}) of data the data warehouse is expected to grow to hold 27 terabytes of data.

Analysts have access to at least 14 months' data regarding profitability, house-holding and demographics about First Union's customers. This data is analysed using sophisticated third-party decision support and data-mining tools such as SAS, Business Objects, MicroStrategy's DSS Suite and Prime Response's Vantage. Apart from using simple browsers to access the data the decision maker can access and manipulate the data using four other interfaces – Sigma Executive, Sigma Explorer, Sigma Prospector and Sigma Analyst.

Sigma Executive offers the decision maker basic reports, such as pie charts and simple visuals. Sigma Explorer is similar to Sigma Executive, but offers many more reporting options that provide detailed data-analysis capabilities. Sigma Prospector is a campaign-management tool, which is ideal for customer relationship marketing and lead distribution/list building. Sigma Analyst provides the highest level of detail and allows for sophisticated and intricate transaction data reporting, analysis and data mining.

According to Naras Eechambadi, 'People are practically breaking down the doors to get access to the data mart. Just by pointing and clicking, analysts can get in a few seconds what used to take a few days, and sometimes weeks. If we realise even a fraction of what's possible . . . the system will have paid for itself several times over.' He further goes on to say, 'Having the data, the intelligence, the processes, and the models helps us be more accurate than we would be otherwise. In general, we have doubled and tripled our average response to direct mail campaigns across the board.'

References

Applegate, A., Konsynski, B. and Nunamaker, J. (1986) Model management systems: Design for decision support, *Decision Support Systems*, **2**, 81–91.

Carroll, J. M. (1995) Introduction: The scenario perspective on system development, in J. M. Carroll (ed.), *Scenario Based Design: Envisioning Work and Technology in System Development*, John Wiley and Sons, New York, pp. 1–19.

Geoffrion, A. (1992) The SML language for structured modeling: Levels 1 and 2, *Operations Research*, **40**(1).

Hamacher, S. (1995) *Modeling systems for operations research problems: Study and applications*, Ph.D. Dissertation, Industrial Engineering, Ecole Paris Centrale, Paris, 235 pp.

Kim, W. (1996) Object-relational database technology, *UniSql Whitepaper*.

Kottemann, J. E. and Dolk, D. R. (1992) Model integration and modeling languages: A process perspective, *Information Systems Research*, **3**(1), 1–16.

Smith, J. M., and Smith, D. C. P. (1977) Database abstractions: Aggregation and generalization, *ACM Transactions on Database Systems*, **2**(2), 105–133.

Stonebraker, M. and Moore, D. (1996) *Object-Relational DBMS's: The Next Great Wave*, Morgan Kaufmann Publishers, Inc., San Francisco, California.

DISCUSSION QUESTIONS

1. Keeping in mind the four key functional extensions that object-relational systems provide, remodel a relational database application that you are familiar with to provide rich decision support capability.

2. Consider the object classes 'person' and 'department' in the context of an organisation. How would you model them to provide rich decision support using the object-relational features discussed in this chapter?

3. Compare object-relational systems with other database systems that you are familiar with in terms of their ability
   - to manage complex data;
   - to provide for utilising models (such as optimisation);
   - to provide an effective user interface.

4. Discuss the ways in which object-relational systems are similar to and different from object-oriented programming systems. Readers unfamiliar with the latter would benefit greatly from reading a basic book on object-oriented programming and putting it in the context of the material discussed in this book.

6

A Visual Approach to Problem Analysis

6.1 Introduction

Throughout the book, we have stressed the importance of analysing problems by examining data and modelling aspects somewhat simultaneously. This is important to address important aspects of the problem that may depend on both of these aspects. In Chapter 3 we also introduced some basic aspects of visually dealing with these aspects of problems. In this chapter we will focus exclusively on this notion of visualisation as an effective means by which we can address the issue of designing applications of the sort that we are discussing in this book. Usually, when we talk about visualising data (in its original or manipulated form), we immediately think of various graphical representations of numerical data. Hence, we can argue that in many cases it may make sense to display some numerical data – such as sales distributions – over time using a graph, as opposed to displaying those numbers in the tabular form. This issue becomes all the more important when we consider applications with vast volumes of data where the appropriate display of information is at least as important as the methods by which appropriate data ought to be extracted. As we have seen in some of the examples in Chapter 3, this notion of useful ways of displaying data has been built into many of the more commonly used technologies. For our purposes, we want to go beyond the basic issue of how best to display data – the output side of the equation. We also want to investigate the technologies that enable us to specify how data needs to be accessed and manipulated in order to produce the output that we want as problem solvers. In other words, visualisation, as we consider it in this chapter, looks at both the input and the output sides of application use.

6.2 Basic Issues

One of the essential components of a decision support system is a good dialogue interface that provides ready access to system contents. Over the last few years, considerable research attention has focused on this issue of interface design and ways by which its quality may be improved. Researchers such as Tufte (1997) and Norman and Draper (1986) have discussed issues relating to user interfaces, their effectiveness and design strategies for enhancing the visual portrayal of complex information. An important outcome of this effort is the development in visual interface technologies that allow for the direct manipulation of system objects (e.g. Glinert, 1990). Direct manipulation refers to the ability of the user to interact with the contents of an application in a graphical manner. This is in contrast to the many examples that we have seen thus far where a command-language-oriented approach has been used. Such an approach requires that the user translate the task requirements into the syntax

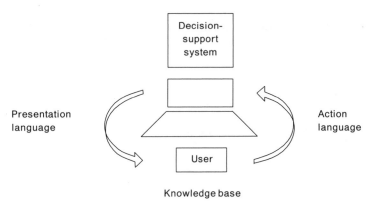

Figure 6.1. Presentation and action languages.

demanded by the textual command-oriented language. A graphical user interface designed by the principles of visualisation and direct manipulation is a useful feature for good decision support.

There are two major components in a typical user interface – the presentation language and the action language. The presentation language encompasses the methods used by the system to display system outputs to the user. The action language, on the other hand, focuses on the methods available to the user to instruct the system to perform certain actions. The user brings to bear background knowledge about the task domain in constructing these action specifications. These ideas are depicted in Figure 6.1.

A utility of visually driving the action and the presentation languages is to enable the user to express requirements in a more 'natural' fashion. These ideas have been expressed rather succinctly by Norman and Draper (1986) who referred to the semantic distance between a typical user and the application system. The emphasis was on the need to make system artefacts fit the needs of human problem solvers. Ease of interaction depends on the cognitive effort demanded of the user to map task requirements with those of the physical system. Hence, any design principle that made such mapping easier would be worth pursuing. The successful implementation of this approach must contribute to the bridging of the gulf between what the user wants to accomplish and what the system demands in order to approach user goals. The purpose of leveraging visualisation concepts to address this semantic distance is to reduce the gulf of execution and evaluation between user goals and the state of the physical system. Users would benefit greatly from being able to use visually oriented techniques to express execution requirements and evaluate presentations from the system. Figure 6.2 captures these ideas.

Interaction with the system is what enables the user to describe a problem and produce meaningful results through the specification of a sequence of actions. These actions may make reference to the diversity of data by specifying the need to view any

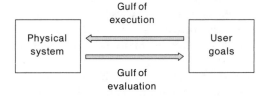

Figure 6.2. Gulf of execution and evaluation (Norman and Draper, 1986).

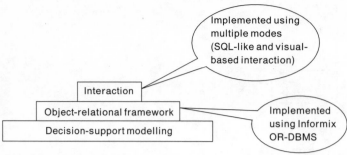

Figure 6.3. A layered framework for modelling.

meaningful part of it; alternatively, a collection of models specifying particular types of manipulation (along with the data that will be manipulated) may be specified. In either case, the flow of interaction should be uniform so that the specification of what a user wants to accomplish can be accommodated within a common framework. A visualisation focus to specifying actions is seen as a powerful way by which a wider community of users may be included in their ability to participate in the design and use of such applications. Visually driven interaction is typically easier to use compared with text-oriented interaction; the persistent debate is whether the two approaches are comparable in terms of expressive power.

Figure 6.3 shows a layered approach that we adopt to the analysis and design of DSS applications. This conceptualisation of the modelling environment illustrates where visualisation fits in to the overall architecture of DSS design. A typical application domain is characterised as being complex because of a combination of factors. The data that describes an instance of the problem, in addition to being voluminous, is made up of complex structures. Furthermore, interaction between the data and a need for managing it for problem solving require a well-organised strategy for conceptualising and implementing an application. Manipulation of the data may be required as per one or more manipulation rules. These rules may range from simple algebraic expressions to complex algorithms.

An object-relational platform for implementation offers us a development platform that is well suited to the needs of such applications. Typically, these needs include the management of complex data and the provision to integrate these complex objects. Such a platform is uniquely capable of meeting the conceptual requirements while satisfying many practical design concerns such as performance, persistence and interoperability. We approach the interface issue by examining multiple 'levels' of interaction – associative language (such as SQL) and visually driven. The main benefit of approaching the design problem via this framework is that it allows us to build a progressive map from the problem domain to the design product. By doing so, we can logically locate visually driven processes within an overall context of DSS design.

In the rest of this chapter, we focus on two specific design approaches to addressing the visualisation issue. The first approach leverages the benefits of the object-relational framework that we used in the previous chapter which offers us many benefits to tackle complex problems. The second approach focuses on incremental application building to address a series of task requirements in the context of a particular problem domain. In both cases, we emphasise the visually driven support of the application development process, although we use several examples of alternative display choices.

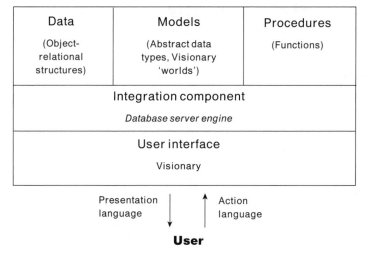

Data	Models	Procedures
(Object-relational structures)	(Abstract data types, Visionary 'worlds')	(Functions)

Integration component

Database server engine

User interface

Visionary

Presentation language ↓ ↑ Action language

User

Figure 6.4. DSS Architecture with reference to Visionary.

6.3 The Visionary Approach

We briefly introduced Visionary, the visual aspect of the object-relational DBMS Informix, in Chapter 3. The main motivation for an environment like Visionary is to allow the user to visually express task requirements without sacrificing the underlying power of a powerful database engine. In the case of Visionary, all the benefits of an object-relational database are retained while employing the visualisation of user specification of tasks. Figure 6.4 shows how visualisation is implemented in Visionary within the overall context of a typical DSS architecture.

The object-relational database engine provides typical database services. It supports traditional and complex data and allows the specification of functions using a variety of methods. It also allows the user specification by building a task definition showing the process flows involved in going from basic application components to end results. Visionary uses the notion of a 'world' to refer to such a depiction.

6.3.1 The Product Sales Forecasting Problem Revisited

We continue with the problem that we introduced in the previous chapter regarding the forecasting of demand for products in a typical production environment. The problem centres around the generation of accurate forecasts of product sales. Complications arise because of certain standard ways of characterising the environment. Products are made up of several items and therefore the generation of a product-level forecast usually involves generating item-level forecasts and then aggregating them accordingly. Furthermore, as we saw in the previous chapter, there are several available methods to generate forecasts using historical data. We want the user to be able to flexibly use one or more of the available methods depending on the circumstances in order to generate satisfactory results. We assume that historical sales data and the various forecasting functions have been defined in an Informix database application as per the guidelines described in the previous chapter.

We focus now on how the visual interface can be used to address specific tasks within this context.

6.3.2 Modelling Support Using a Visually Driven Approach

Visionary allows both casual non-technical end-users and experienced developers to build complete applications without writing a single line of code. The user specification takes the form of a flow diagram that depicts the transitions from sources of data to desired outputs. The diagram is in the form of boxes that show objects of various sorts and connecting arrows that show transitory flows. The objects represented in the boxes are selected from a panel of object types. These types may consist of simple or complex and constructed datatypes, or functions that can manipulate the data. They in turn make reference to instances that are defined as part of an Informix database using traditional definition approaches described in the previous chapter. Data that is not resident as part of the application may also be included in the construction. This allows the inclusion of specific data for which there is no requirement that it persists as part of the database. The result is a user-created 'program' which Visionary calls a 'world'. The concept of a world allows users to build a task scenario on demand as opposed to constructing text-based queries. Any number of such worlds may be created and stored as part of the application to be recalled on demand. Figure 6.5 shows the inputs and outputs of the process described above.

There are two key areas in the Visionary modelling environment:

1. The Ingredient/Reusable Model Component Area shows all the available ingredients/ reusable model components that the modeller/decision maker can use in the specification of a task scenario (a world). The ingredients are the building blocks that can be dragged onto the panel where the user's specification is being constructed. The following are the significant items that are included in the set of ingredients from which the user may choose specific items:
   - Tables contain data that describe task instances.
   - Functions are actions that have been defined and stored as part of the application. They operate on the data contained in tables.
   - Constants provide values for parameters if needed in defining a particular scenario.
   - Run-time values allow the specification of particular values at the point in time when a scenario is evaluated through execution.
   - Filters allow the specification and use of data-selection criteria.
   - Graphic allows the specification of how execution results should be displayed.
   - Query allows the option of using extensions of the SQL language to define a scenario as an alternative form of visually driven definitions.
2. The Modelling/Scenario Generation Area is where ingredients/reusable model components are linked using the box-and-arrow paradigm. The ingredients/reusable model components are the boxes and these are linked using arrows that indicate the flow of information between model components.

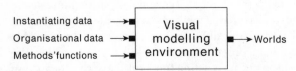

Figure 6.5. Visionary's visual modelling environment.

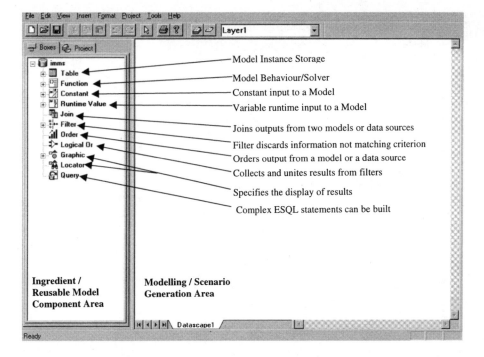

Figure 6.6. Components of a Visionary world construction panel.

Figure 6.6 shows a screen image of the two areas on a Visionary panel as described above.

6.3.3 Scenario Specification

We now proceed to show how specific tasks associated with the product forecasting application can be addressed in the Visionary environment. We do this by considering a series of typical tasks that constitute a decision support process in this application domain.

6.3.3.1 Using Historical Data to Generate Forecasts

Historical data about sales of products is contained in a table that is stored as part of the application. Typically, this contains both simple and complex data because of the inherent nature of the application. At a particular point in time, the data contained in such a table may be considered as an instance of the forecasting model of the problem. In other words, it represents the data describing the problem at a particular point in time. A procedure to manipulate the data can be defined and stored as a function. Sometimes, such a procedure may be referred to as a *solver* implying that it can be called upon to produce 'solved' results using the data that describe the problem at hand. In our situation, an example of such a solver is the procedure that uses multiple regression, a statistical technique, to produce forecasts. The specification of such a solver was described in the previous chapter. Here, we assume that it is available and can be put to use if necessary. The data input to the solver (historical sales) needs to be specified. Furthermore, the manner in which the results of using the solver – the forecasts – needs to be displayed and should be specified. Figure 6.7 below shows the constructed scenario to carry out this task. Note that the

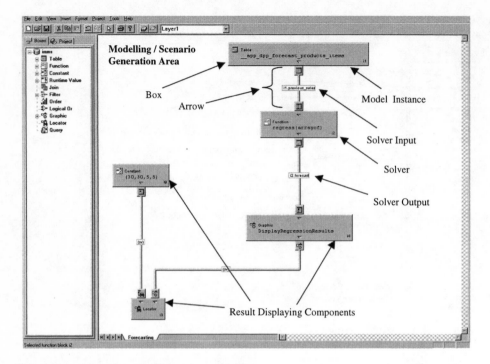

Figure 6.7. Generating sales forecasts using Visionary.

elements of the scenario are built up using the ingredients selected appropriately from the choice list in the selection area.

Each link that connects boxes is annotated appropriately to indicate what data flows from one box to the next. The output of the solver which contains the forecasts is routed to a locator box with required specifications through a display control so that the results are displayed in a manner chosen by the user. Such a display could be one of several possible graphical displays (as is the case in this example) or a tabular display. These same components could be linked in different configurations, giving rise to a variety of modelling scenarios. Visionary uses typing as a mechanism to ensure only valid connections are made between model components. The types of the data sources to a function should match the input types defined for that function. If the user connects model components whose types do not match, Visionary invalidates the modelling scenario. A completed scenario is executed in order to produce the desired results. It may be saved and recalled as part of the application if so desired by the user.

6.3.3.2 Using Multiple Solvers: Consolidation

There are many situations where a user might want to try different approaches to manipulate the data to produce a particular result. In this example, multiple regression is just one possible technique for generating sales forecasts. An alternative technique that we might want to investigate is the use of exponential smoothing – another common forecasting method. In a manner similar to the regression solver, the exponential smoothing method may also be defined as a new solver (function) in the application. It is now possible to investigate a newly generated sales forecast by consolidating the results

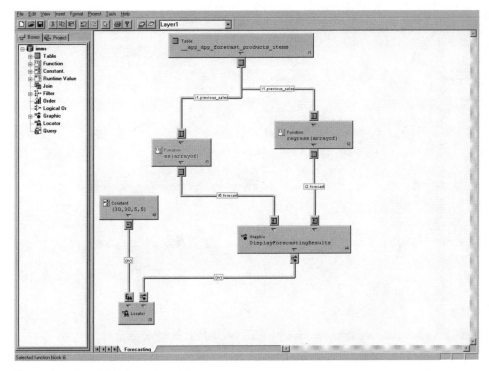

Figure 6.8. Consolidation of models.

from the two forecasting methods. Figure 6.8 shows a Visionary screen shot of such a definition.

Note that the source table provides the same data input (historical sales) to both the regression and the exponential smoothing functions. The results are then appropriately consolidated as part of the display definition. This process can also be viewed as the integration of two different modelling scenarios – one using exponential smoothing and the other regression.

6.3.3.3 Using Multiple Solvers: Pipelining

A different modelling approach to using solvers is to link multiple solvers in linear fashion. For example, it is common to use a forecast to generate a sales plan. In this example, we want to combine a sales forecast using one of several possible forecasting methods with a solver that can calculate the effective demand for the product. The latter solver uses a method that combines the forecast with existing product inventory and other relevant data to produce the effective demand for the subsequent time period. Here the output of the solver that does the forecast is used as the input to the solver that computes the effective demand for the product. Again, we assume the solvers have been defined and stored as part of the application. Figure 6.9 shows how the pipelining scenario is specified.

The first solver (function regress) regresses on past sales and produces a forecast that becomes the input to the second solver (function cal_eff_dem) that calculates the effective demand. Though only two solvers are shown in this example, there could be more than two solvers. The pipelining scenarios could be more complex involving more models in different configurations.

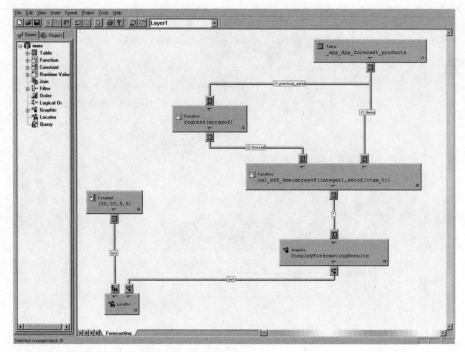

Figure 6.9. Pipelining of solvers.

6.3.3.4 Flexible Scenario Generation: Doing 'What-if' Analysis

A common aspect of decision support tasks is to examine the sensitivity of certain results to changes in input assumptions. In Chapter 4 we saw some examples of doing sensitivity analysis in the context of examining promotion effectiveness. The typical approach to doing sensitivity analysis is to ask the question, "What if this specific change was made." In other words, what is the effect on results if a particular change was made on the input side of the task definition. In the Visionary environment, the ingredient called 'Run-time Values' is particularly useful for generating such flexible problem scenarios to reflect task requirements. Figure 6.10 shows the use of this ingredient to build a specification to carry out this analysis.

The exponential smoothing forecast solver uses a parameter called Alpha in order to generate forecasts. The particular value that the parameter takes on reflects the user's understanding of the application domain and has a noticeable effect on the results. This is a classic situation where the user might want to see the forecasts generated for a series of scenarios, each of which have a different parameter Alpha value. In this example, the particular value is provided at the time of execution of the scenario as input into the function using the Run-time Value ingredient. In other words, the question that is being asked here is the following, "What if the Alpha value was set at some chosen level." This analysis could be repeated an arbitrary number of times with the actual value of Alpha changing at each iteration.

6.3.4 The Utility of a Visionary-like Environment for Decision Support

The Visionary modelling environment allows the decision maker to carry out complex decision modelling tasks with relative ease. Visionary provides an environment that allows

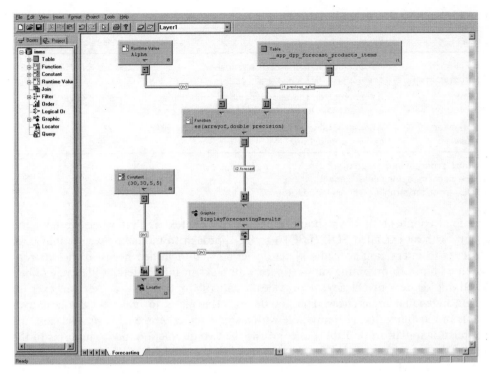

Figure 6.10. 'What-if' analysis.

modellers and decision makers to create, manipulate and execute complex modelling scenarios. It also reduces the cognitive load on the decision maker by automatically taking over tasks such as modelling-scenario validation, displaying information relating to the available model-instance storage structures/tables, available procedures/functions, etc. Visionary's environment enhances the reuse of modelling components by allowing the decision maker to use the same components in a variety of modelling scenarios. Modelling scenarios could be executed dynamically as they are created or they can be saved and used at a later date. The Visionary environment allows the decision maker to conduct extensive what-if/sensitivity analyses through the use of run-time values, consolidation and multiple modelling scenarios.

In discussing Visionary as a useful environment in which to conduct decision support activities, we give due recognition to the possibility that the interaction needs of different users may vary substantially. For example, we may distinguish among the needs of a decision maker, a model builder and a programmer, all of whom may legitimately interact with the application. Stonebraker and Moore (1996) use the corresponding descriptive terms for these user roles – end-user, little-programmer and big-programmer. The skills required of these roles and their modes of interaction with the system are shown in Table 6.1. The information contained in the table is a useful way to think about the role of visually driven modelling in the context of user skills. While visual modelling does not negate the need for other development paradigms, it addresses an important aspect of design related to a diverse community of users. In some cases, complex manipulation solvers may be best dealt with in a programming language such as C. In other cases, extended SQL-type syntax will have a dominant role, as seen in the previous chapter. In other cases, a Visionary-type interface will go a long way in encouraging productive development work among a greater number of users.

Table 6.1. User roles and modes of interaction.

User role	Skills	Modes of interaction
Programmer (big programmer)	A sophisticated C and ESQL application developer	C*, ESQL*** and VME**
Model builder (little programmer)	A sophisticated end-user capable of constructing applications in an end-user programming system	ESQL and VME
Decision maker (end-user)	A non-programmer who primarily runs a previously defined application.	VME

*   C – the C programming language.
**   VME – visual modelling environment.
*** ESQL – extended structured query language.

The final comment that we should make in this context is that when we compare Visionary with an extended SQL (ESQL) based approach to modelling we see that both approaches to interaction with the system cater to well-identified needs in the environment. In addition to providing support across all tasks in the modelling life cycle (albeit with varying degrees of efficacy) it provides a valuable option that a user can exercise based on individual preferences. The key design principle is to make these alternatives available in a manner that is compatible with a single underlying engine (in this case, the object-relational platform). Table 6.2 contrasts the two interaction modes in terms of the nature of the support provided for various tasks in the modelling life cycle. The ESQL environment is useful in terms of its ability to support many parts of the modelling life cycle effectively. However, the many compelling reasons that we have discussed make it important to offer the visually driven alternative. In many cases, it is the useful first step before use of the application is possible at all.

6.4 The Clementine Approach

Clementine (Integral Solutions Limited) offers a toolkit whose visual programming interface allows accessing, manipulating and experimenting with data, and testing out hypotheses. The user selects, manipulates and links together icons to form different scenarios. Icons could connect to databases, manipulate and derive new data, train neural nets, build rules from data, plot graphs, histograms, and data webs, regress on data, equalise distributions, etc. Icons are selected from a palette, placed on a drawing board, and connected using arrows to form modelling scenarios. These scenarios are executed to produce output in the form of rules, predictions, graphs, models, etc. Clementine supports most parts of the modelling life cycle well but restricts itself to data-mining algorithms. We conclude that Clementine offers a useful visually oriented environment that could be used productively for decision support applications. We saw a few simple examples of using Clementine in Chapter 3. Here, as with the Visionary exposition in this chapter, we discuss the use of Clementine in the context of a particular problem domain and in dealing with a series of specific tasks in that domain.

6.4.1 Examining Potential Customer Data

Consider the example that we discussed in Chapter 1 about Merrill Lynch's desire to understand their existing and potential customers better in order to attract potential clients. The decision process in such an environment starts typically by examining data

Table 6.2. Modelling life-cycle tasks.

Modelling tasks	ESQL	Visual modelling
Model Formulation	Formulation of base models as well as complex models	Formulation of complex models from base models
Model instantiation	Direct as well as indirect instantiation	Parameter instantiation
Model-data integration	Cumbersome ESQL syntax	Menus and icons
Model-solver integration	Cumbersome ESQL syntax	Menus and icons
Model storage	Allows storage of base models and complex models but not of modelling scenarios	Allows the storage of modelling scenarios
Model termination	Termination of base and complex models	Termination of only modelling scenarios
Model integrity/validity checks	Rules and strong typing allows us to check the integrity of model instances	Strong typing allow us to check the validity of complex models
Model execution	Well supported	Well supported
Model reformation	Complex model reformulation supported but limited support for base model reformulation	Complex models/modelling scenarios reformulation supported
What-if analysis capabilities	Well supported but cumbersome ESQL syntax	Well supported
Levels of integration		
Aggregation	Well supported but cumbersome ESQL syntax	Well supported
Pipelining	Well supported but cumbersome ESQL syntax	Well supported
Splicing	Well supported but cumbersome ESQL syntax	Well supported
Types of integration		
Permanent integration	Well supported but cumbersome ESQL syntax	Not supported
Ad hoc integration	Well supported but cumbersome ESQL syntax	Well supported

about existing and potential customers to try and discover useful patterns in the data. Usually, this means that we want to display the data using a variety of graphical formats to see if they expose any relationships between customer characteristics. Alternatively, we may use models of various types to analyse the data to see if relationships that are not obvious emerge from the analysis. Data about *existing* customers usually exists in an organisational database. Data about *potential* customers have to be obtained from other sources outside the organisation. In the Merrill Lynch example the company used a combination of their own data and data that was acquired from a third party in order to identify high potential clients.

In this section we use a dataset, compiled by the United States Census Bureau, that is reported by researchers working in areas that address the issue of examining relationships in large datasets (e.g. Kohavi, 1996). Specifically, we use data about adults engaged in work that describes their level of education, hours of work per week, compensation, etc. The decision problem involves investigation of this dataset for two fundamental sets of activities:

- What are the characteristics of the data that describe individuals and how can they be displayed visually in order to highlight important characteristics of the data?

Table 6.3. The adult database description.

Attribute	Description
age	Continuous variable – numeric
education-num	Continuous variable – number of years of education
sex	Female, male
capital-gain	Continuous variable – increase in individual's capital
capital-loss	Continuous variable – decrease in individual's capital
hours-per-week	Continuous variable – hours per week of work
class	2-category variable >50K, $\leq$50K – annual salary

- How can the data be usefully analysed to understand relationships between important subsets of the dataset?

The dataset contains a number of attributes that are descriptive of a set of working adults. We were interested in analysing particular variables related to economic issues. Specifically, we wanted to examine possible relationships between descriptive variables and compensation for work. To do this we used a subset of the census data consisting of 32,500 records as a starting point and focused on the attributes of interest to our application. Table 6.3 shows what these attributes are and the nature of the data values that occur.

6.4.2 Visual Modelling

As was the case with Visionary, there are two aspects of visually based modelling in the Clementine context. The first is the specification by the user (the action language) of the task requirements; the second is the presentation of the results in an appropriate format. Although our focus is on the former since this is the focus of this chapter, we also include an example of the latter since that is appropriate in the context of the examples that we present. Clementine follows an approach that is similar to Visionary in the following sense: there is a panel from which building blocks or ingredients can be selected and placed on a blank panel where the specification is constructed. The main difference between Clementine and Visionary is that the set of choices from the ingredients list is larger in variety. However, the full-blown support of database issues that is available in the Visionary environment (through its link with the Informix database management system) is absent in the Clementine environment.

Task specification in Clementine involves the construction of a *stream* of objects chosen from the selection panel and linked appropriately by directed arrows. The specification must involve the three broad categories of inputs (sources of data for the task), transformations (manipulation of the input data) and outputs (the results of the manipulation). Defined streams can be named and stored for reuse if necessary. A complete stream can be submitted for execution (by clicking on an appropriate button) and the results can be viewed based on the output specification of the stream. As is the case with Visionary, the appeal of task specification using this paradigm is the ability of the user to construct the stream entirely in a visual manner.

6.4.3 Stream Construction and Execution

We now proceed with a series of examples showing how Clementine can be used to address specific task requirements within the overall context of the adult database described earlier. Many of these tasks reflect the need of the user to examine the nature of the data and to explore relationships between different aspects of the data. The perspective that the application takes is similar to the Merrill Lynch example where the idea was to be able to realise some broad patterns that could then be followed up as necessary on an individual basis.

6.4.3.1 Creating the Data Source For the Application

Recall that we said that we will use a subset of the dataset in developing our application. The first step in the process is to prepare an appropriate subset for further analysis. This means that we need to specify the specific variables that we will use and how specific records will be chosen for the analysis. The result of this exercise is the creation of a table that contains data which can be used as the source for further analysis. The specification stream in order to do this is shown in Figure 6.11a. The stream shows that the file containing the raw data has to be filtered in order to first indicate the specific variables that we are interested in for further analysis. A sample drawn from 50 percent of the raw data is then used with the chosen variable set to produce the table. The table is just one format for the output data. It allows us to examine the data in tabular form. As we will see a number of alternative formats for viewing and using the same output data are available as well.

Figures 6.11b and 6.11c show the filtering and sample selection details that need to be specified as part of the stream construction process. These details are provided by highlighting each object on the panel and then entering the required information. As far as the filtering specification is concerned, the attributes to be included in the final analysis are selected from the raw list by clicking on each one. Only the selected attributes will show up in the result. The specification regarding row selection indicates that the table for analysis should contain 1,000 rows. These will be selected randomly from 50 percent of the raw dataset. The reason for this is that it allows us to conduct an analysis on part of the dataset and hold back the remainder to test model results with. When this stream is executed, the output is a table, the contents of which correspond to the filtering and sampling specifications included as part of the stream. Figure 6.11d shows what this table will look like.

6.4.3.2 Examining the Strength of Relationships

In this example we now want to use the data that is contained in the table that was created as the output of the stream. However, we want to display the data in a way that allows us to address a selection of hypotheses about the relationships between selected variables. In

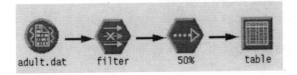

Figure 6.11a. Creating the data source.

Figure 6.11b. Filtering the raw data.

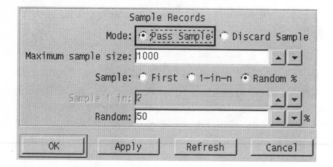

Figure 6.11c. Specifying the sample for analysis.

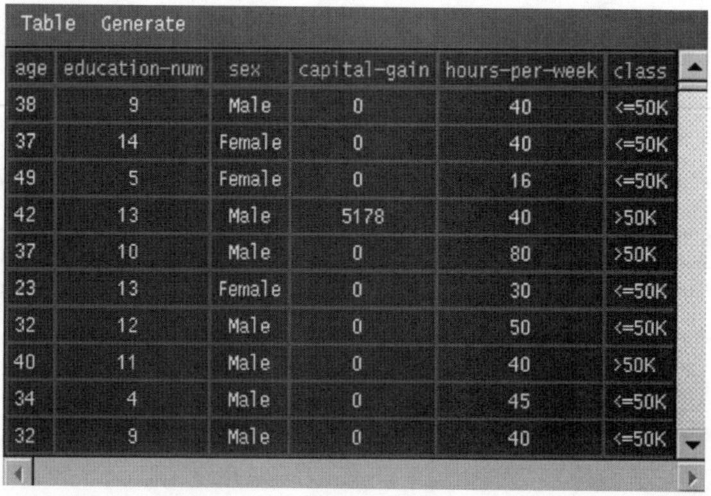

age	education-num	sex	capital-gain	hours-per-week	class
38	9	Male	0	40	<=50K
37	14	Female	0	40	<=50K
49	5	Female	0	16	<=50K
42	13	Male	5178	40	>50K
37	10	Male	0	80	>50K
23	13	Female	0	30	<=50K
32	12	Male	0	50	<=50K
40	11	Male	0	40	>50K
34	4	Male	0	45	<=50K
32	9	Male	0	40	<=50K

Figure 6.11d. The result of stream execution.

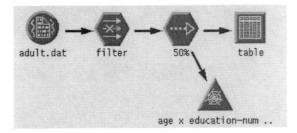

Figure 6.12a. Inclusion of network modelling.

Web Details

Web fields: age / education—num / sex / capital—gain

Select None   Select All

Only true values for flags: ☐

Thresholds are: Absolute

Show only connections of: 40   ▲ ▼ and above

Weak connections below: 60   ▲ ▼

Strong connections above: 80   ▲ ▼

Discard if very few records: ☐ Min records/line: 2   ▲ ▼

Discard if very many records: ☐ Max records/line: 10000   ▲ ▼

| OK | Execute | Apply | Refresh | Cancel |

Figure 6.12b. Specification details for network modelling.

this case the hypotheses refer to the key attributes that are related to salary – age, gender (sex) and years of education. While there are a number of statistical methods that can be used to test these hypotheses, Clementine offers a simple yet powerful visual approach to doing this. It creates a network (also referred to as a web) of relationships between selected variables and displays relative strengths of these relationships. This is one of several graphical-display formats that can be used to explore the dataset. We approach this problem by incrementally modifying the existing Clementine stream to add this display. Figure 6.12a shows the modified stream. The additional node in the stream is an output node chosen from a graphical display suite. The data that will be included in the display will be identical to that contained in the table as indicated by the location of the link to the graphical display.

Figure 6.12b shows the specification of the details for the display. Specifically, the user must specify the attributes (variables) that should be included in the display. In this example, the chosen attributes are age, sex, years of education and class (salary grouping). These are selected by clicking on the appropriate attributes from a selection list based on the source for the display. A network diagram counts the frequency of association between every pair of values of the chosen attributes. The specification panel can be used to

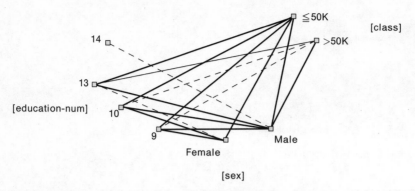

Figure 6.12c. Execution results for network modelling.

indicate the threshold for the strengths of the relationships for inclusion in the network. In this case the user's strength specifications are as follows:

- Display only those relationships that have a frequency of at least 40 connections.
- Classify relationships as weak, moderate or strong, based on the frequency of connections using 40, 60 and 80 respectively as the cut-off values.

Figure 6.12c shows the display as per these specifications. Execution of this stream results in the generation of this figure. Dotted connections show weak relationships, ordinary lines show moderate relationships and heavy lines show strong relationships. The following observations can be made by examining the network display:

- There are between 40 and 60 men in the dataset with 14 years of education.
- There are between 60 and 80 individuals in the dataset who have 13 years of education and earn over $50K per year.
- There are over 80 women who earn less than $50K per year.
- There are less than 40 women who earn more than $50K per year (this is indicated by the absence of any link between those two attribute values).
- There are less than 40 individuals of any particular age who belong to a single category of any of the other attributes (this is indicated by the fact that, although age was selected from the attribute list based on the hypothesis, it does not show up anywhere in the display).

While all of the above may appear to be simple observations, it should be noted that these are results that are not intuitive, and could not be assessed without some systematic approach. The one used here is a visual-display technique that highlights the nature of these relationships. It is up to the user to use these results appropriately in the decision-making context.

6.4.3.3 Alternative Useful Displays of the Data

Using the network diagram to display relationships of interest is just one of several available formats. Matching the task requirements to an appropriate display format is the challenge faced by the user. For example, the following two tasks may be approached by using appropriate display formats:

- What is the relationship between age and salary grouping? Do the two salary groups contain individuals of all ages? Or do some age groups dominate over others in each of the salary groupings?

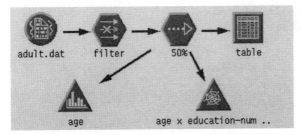

Figure 6.13a. Adding a histogram to the stream.

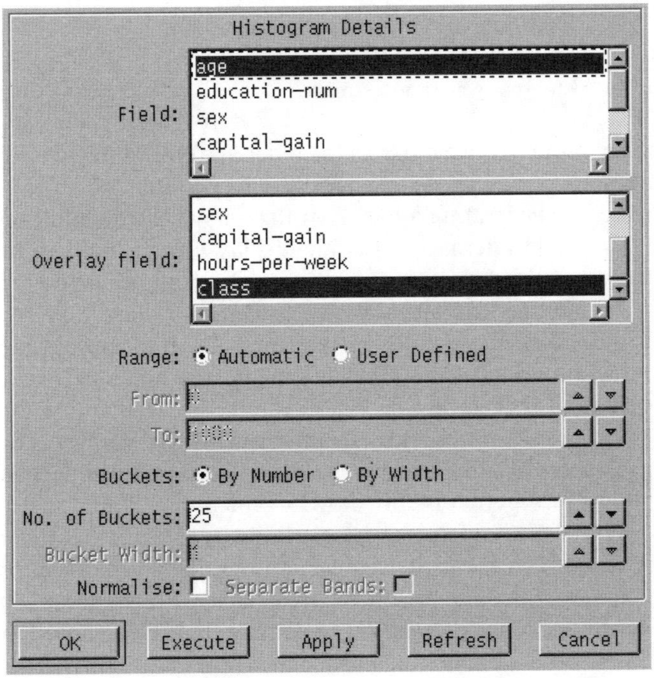

Figure 6.13b. Specification details for the histogram.

- What is the distribution of hours of work in a week across the two genders? Do men (or women) work for a larger (or lower) number of hours per week? How does this distribution present itself over the entire range of hours worked?

One of the ways that we can use to address these tasks is to use Clementine's visual-display alternatives. We do this again by incremental modification of the existing stream. To address the first task, we use a histogram to display the distribution of age with salary grouping data overlaid to give us an indication about the age effect. Figure 6.13a shows the inclusion of the node labelled 'age' to produce the desired graphical output.

Details that are needed for the specification of the histogram's characteristics are specified by selecting the attribute for which the display is generated. Furthermore, the age overlay is also specified by its selection in the overlay section of the panel. The panel that shows these selections is shown in Figure 6.13b. Execution of the appropriate part of the stream now produces the result shown in Figure 6.13c. It shows that the under $50K salary

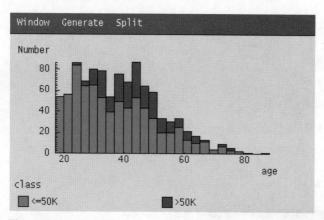

Figure 6.13c. Execution results for the histogram generation stream.

group dominates in the younger age group. As we move to the older age groups, there is an increasing number of individuals who belong to the over $50K salary group.

The second task can be addressed by generating a bar chart that shows the distribution of the hours worked per week. This is an alternative graphic-display format that can be specified by the appropriate addition of the details on the stream. This is indicated by the icon labelled 'hours-per-week'. The modified stream is shown in Figure 6.14a.

As before, specification of the necessary details is indicated by the appropriate selections that are made in a selection panel. Here we want to use the hours-per-week attribute for generating the distribution that we desire. Furthermore, we want to use the gender attribute 'sex' as an overlay to address the issues brought up earlier. The specification details are shown in Figure 6.14b. The execution of this particular part of the stream produces the result shown in Figure 6.14c. It shows us the proportion of males and females in the various categories of the hours-per-week attribute. It appears that there is a greater proportion of males working in the higher values of hour. The proportion of women represented in the lower values of the attribute is relatively higer. Furthermore, 40 hours per week is the most frequently occurring category. The display could be arranged in a number of different sorted orders. For example, this particular display sorts the results based on the frequency of individuals in each category. We could alternatively arrange it by value of the hours-per-week attribute.

Several useful pieces of information can be generated by using appropriate display formats. Again, the inferences drawn from these displays must be applied in a decision-making context by the user.

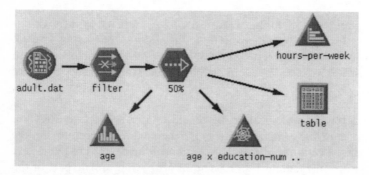

Figure 6.14a. Adding a bar chart to the stream.

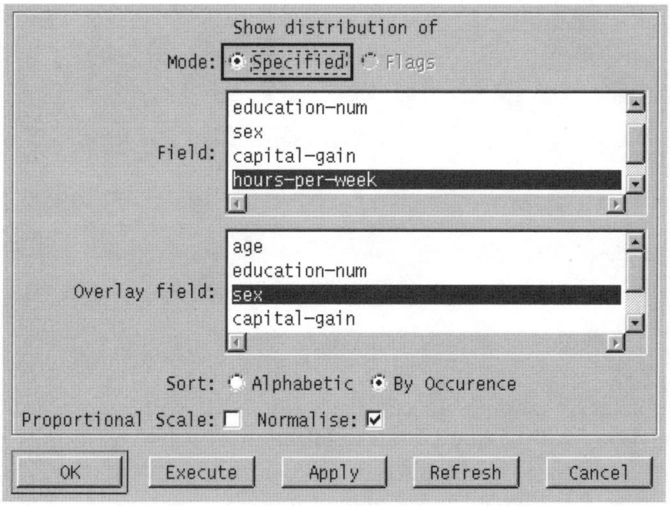

Figure 6.14b. Specification details for the bar chart.

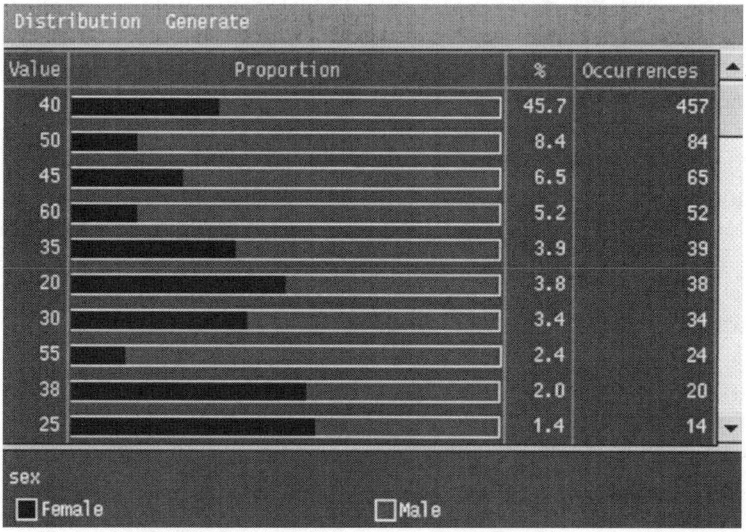

Figure 6.14c. Bar-chart execution results.

6.4.3.4 Using Built-in Models

A useful aspect of an environment like Clementine is that it provides a modelling tool kit to address relationship types of task. While the examples that we have seen thus far allow us to do similar things, it is done by the user who inspects a visual display and draws appropriate conclusions. Some of the modelling techniques that ask similar kinds of questions utilise sophisticated mathematical techniques to generate the required answers. Such an approach will yield results that are more reliable than eyeballing visual displays.

One such modelling approach that Clementine uses analyses the relationships between the variables to see if there are specific reliable combinations of attributes that predict salary grouping. Instead of looking at one attribute at a time, the technique looks at all of

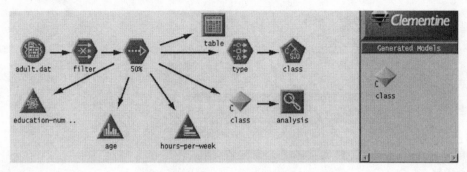

Figure 6.15a. Generating and using built-in modelling capabilities.

the attributes and the existing salary groupings to construct rules that will enable us to predict what group a new individual will belong to. This collection of rules constitutes a classification model instance which can then be applied to newly arriving individuals. The modelling technique is one of several available from a suite of models. Figure 6.15a shows the modification of the stream to include the generation of the classification model instance. This is indicated by the node labelled 'class'. Execution of this part of the stream produces the named model instance called 'class'. The generated model instance is shown in a window on the right of the panel. This model instance actually contains a collection of classification rules that are based on specific attribute values. If necessary, the details of these rules could be displayed as well.

The model instance can now be used to see how well it can predict salary grouping based on data about the contributing variables. This will tell us about the efficacy with which the generated model behaves. This can be analysed by adding an analysis stream that uses a random dataset as input into the model instance. Figure 6.15a also shows this stream with the inclusion of the generated model instance 'class' and the node labelled 'analysis'.

Execution of this part of the stream produces some useful results. It tells us that the classification model instance for this dataset has a 83 per cent accuracy level. In other words, when the generated model was used to 'predict' whether an individual would belong to one or other of the two salary groupings, it did it correctly in 83 per cent of the cases. We know this because we have salary grouping information for our entire dataset. The analysis is a comparison between what the generated model does with what we know to be the actual classification. It is a way by which we can see how good the model instance is before we start using it. Figure 6.15b shows the results of the analysis stream.

6.4.3.5 Linking to External Environments

While there are a limited number of modelling techniques that are built into the Clementine model suite, they are quite powerful in what they can accomplish. Our purpose here is to show the visually driven manner in which complex tasks can be addressed. However, there is always the possibility that users may want to work within a visual specification environment such as Clementine, and yet exploit the power of other special-purpose software environments. Such environments may offer modelling capabilities that Clementine itself does not. One such software environment that is well known for its statistical analysis capabilities is the package called Statistical Programming for the Social Sciences (SPSS).

```
File

Results for output field class
    Comparing $C-class with class
        Correct    :      830     ( 83.00%)
        Wrong      :      170     ( 17.00%)
        Total      :     1000
        Confidence Values Report for $CC-class
            Range                   : 0.5000 - 1.0000
            Mean Correct            : 0.8722
            Mean Incorrect          : 0.7714
            Always Correct Above    : 1.0000 ( 5.2% of cases)
            Always Incorrect Below  : 0.5000 ( 0.1% of cases)
            90.1% accuracy above    : 0.8205
            2.0 fold correct above  : 0.8205 (91.6% accuracy)
```

Figure 6.15b. The performance of the model instance for classification.

The classification problem described above, that calls for the prediction of salary-group affiliation, is handled well by SPSS using a statistical modelling technique called discriminant analysis. This technique combines input variables in particular ways to discover the most effective manner by which we can predict which group an individual belongs to. It is different from the built-in Clementine model that does the classification in the way in which the prediction is done. In this context, it is sufficient for us to say that it uses a sophisticated statistical technique to arrive at its conclusions. Clementine allows the specification of a link into an external environment like SPSS by adding it to a stream. Figure 6.16a shows the modified stream to include the link that is labelled 'SPSS Discriminant'.

Execution of this part of the stream transfers the interaction environment into SPSS where details of the discriminant analysis procedure may be specified. Here, we want to indicate what the grouping variable is (salary) and what the predicting variables are (age, years of education and hours per week). These essential specifications are shown in the panel in Figure 6.16b. The execution of this particular definition of the task is performed by SPSS. The results that are generated can be viewed within either the SPSS or the Clementine environment. Here we show some excerpts which are the essential parts of the output that SPSS generates for the classification problem. Readers familiar with statistical packages like SPSS will recognise the entries in the SPSS display shown in Figure 6.16c.

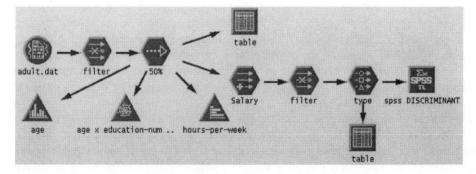

Figure 6.16a. Linking to SPSS.

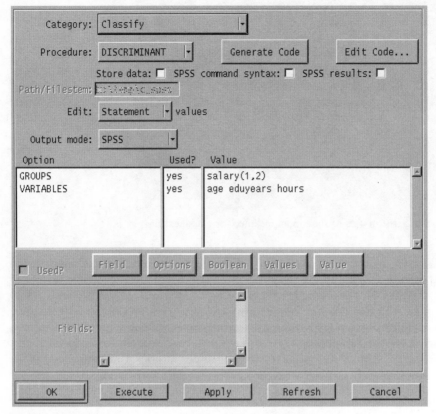

Figure 6.16b. Specifying input details for SPSS discriminant analysis.

6.5 Conclusion

In this chapter we have focused on a visual approach to designing decision support applications. We did this by looking at specific examples from two visualisation platforms – Visionary and Clementine. While Visionary primarily supports an under-lying database application built on an object-relational engine, Clementine offers a more general-purpose modelling capability. The idea behind visualisation is that it is relatively easier for end-users to directly manipulate and interpret iconic representations of problems than to use a constrained text-oriented environment. The emphasis of many commonly used applications has been to focus on visualisation at the output end of applications. In other words, visualisation has focused on how to appropriately display information. While this is an important perspective on visualisation, something that is at least as important is to consider the role of visualisation in the input side of application development. This has to do with how users specify what needs to be done as opposed to how the information is displayed.

In the context of decision support applications, visualization at the specification side of development must be able to deal with the twin aspects of data and manipulation models. In other words, users must be able to specify in iconic style the use of simple and complex data and invoke manipulation methods that interact with data. This visually driven specification is in sharp contrast with more traditional approaches to specification using

Summary of canonical discriminant functions

Eigenvalues

Function	Eigenvalue	% of variance	Cumulative (%)	Canonical Correlation
1	.234[a]	100.0	100.0	.436

[a] First 1 canonical discriminant functions were used in the analysis.

Wilks' lambda

Test of Functions(a)	Wilks' lambda	Chi-square	df	Sig.
1	.810	209.842	3	.000

Standardised canonical discriminant function coefficients

	Function
	1
AGE	.520
EDUYEARS	.684
HOURS	.504

Structure matrix

	Function
	1
EDUYEARS	.689
HOURS	.592
AGE	.443

Pooled within-group correlations between discriminating variables and standardised canonical discriminant functions. Variables ordered by absolute size of correlation within function.

Functions at group centroids

SALARY	Function
	1
1	.281
2	.833

Unstandardised canonical discriminant functions evaluated at group means.

Figure 6.16c. Excerpt from SPSS output.

command languages of various sorts. This is not to say that those languages have no purpose. The important lesson to be learnt is that visually driven interaction will encourage a wider community of users to participate in application development for task exploration and associated problem solving.

Mini-Case: BT Sales and Marketing: Targeting Profitable Customers

The application described here is a good example of an organisational context where sophisticated analysis on data needs to be performed in a relatively straightforward manner. The choice of a visually oriented tool to conduct such analysis reflects the importance of flexibility in performing data analysis by a community of users with a whole range of computing skills.

[Source: *Data Mining Review*, see * http://www.dmreview.com/]

BT, formerly known as British Telecom, supplies phone and data services at national as well as international level. Though based in the United Kingdom, BT has alliances and joint ventures around the world. Sales of BT are around $29 billion annually. As part of their sales and marketing activities BT need to target customers, especially in the context of direct mail campaigns. BT Sales and Marketing need to target customers with the highest propensity to purchase their products as well as target customers who will give the highest comparative value to BT. BT Sales and Marketing have to develop customer profiles that would help them in targeting customers optimally. Such profiles would not only be useful in current campaigns but also in future ones to improve response rates as well as revenues. Data from a number of sources are used to build these customer profiles – existing customer data, billing data, response and transactional data, product and historical data, etc.

To support the Business Highway direct-mail campaign launched in September 1998, BT used Clementine. As Stephen O'Brien, Senior Consultant of Customer and Campaign Analysis for BT Business Connections Program notes, "We used Clementine 5.0's exploratory data and characteristics analysis capabilities – particularly decision-tree analysis – to examine individual data attributes, such as geographic location and number of phone lines. With Clementine, we were able to evaluate relevant attributes so quickly that we developed satisfactory initial selection target criteria even before completing the actual models. Current results show that our models have improved the response rate to the latest Business Highway campaign by 50 percent." One of the key benefits of using such an environment that was identified was the ability to discover trends in the data gathered from various sources.

Stephen notes that "Clementine's greatest strength is its ease of use for exploratory analysis and visualisation of data. It enables you to discover quickly whether a line of investigation will be worthwhile, thus reducing the cost of failure. In only a few days, you can construct a series of explanatory models based on different algorithms and determine their predictive ability ... Clementine provides a rich set of analytics, including neural networks, graphs, rule-induction models, clustering methods and linear regression models, at a highly reasonable cost ... We believe our cost savings achieved in the Business Highway campaign alone will pay for Clementine quite easily."

Some of the key benefits of visualisation and data-mining environments like Clementine are the insights about data and visual representations of those insights through graphs and models. The powerful yet intuitive user interface of a tool like Clementine guides decision makers through a logical progression in analysis leading to the comment that they can be used even without the documentation.

References

Clementine, see http://www.isl.co.uk/

Glinert, E. P. (1990) *Visual Programming Environments: Applications and Issues*, IEEE Computer Society Press, Los Alamitos, California.

Kohavi, R. (1996) Scaling up the accuracy of Naive-Bayes classifiers: A decision-tree hybrid, *Proceedings of the Second International Conference on Knowledge Discovery and Data Mining, Portland, USA*.

Norman, D. A. and Draper S. W. (eds) (1986) *User Centred System Design: New Perspectives on Human Computer Interaction*, Erlbaum Associates, Hillsdale, USA.

Stonebraker, M. and Moore, D. (1996) *Object-Relational DBMS's: The Next Great Wave*, Morgan Kaufmann Publishers, Inc., San Francisco, California.

Tufte, E. R. (1997) *Visual Explanations: Images and Quantities, Evidence and Narrative*, Graphics Press, Cheshire, USA.

Visionary, see http://www.informix.com

DISCUSSION QUESTIONS

1. Identify the presentation and action languages used in a computer-based information system of your choice.
2. What are the key benefits of using a visually driven decision support environment such as Visionary or Clementine?
3. Describe a decision support situation using the 'boxes and arrows' data flow paradigm of Visionary and the 'streams' data flow paradigm of Clementine.
4. Evaluate a particular decision support technology that you have encountered in terms of its ability to support the modelling life-cycle tasks.
5. Do visually driven decision support environments like Visionary and Clementine obviate the need for programmers and model builders? Discuss both sides of this issue.

7

Data Warehousing, On-Line Analytical Processing and Data Mining

7.1 Introduction

An issue that frequently crops up in the context of IT applications is the overload of information that is presented to the decision maker. In many of the examples that we have discussed thus far, we have emphasised the significant role of data in these applications. Typically, we want to support applications where significant volumes of data is almost always a reality. The natural consequence of this is to examine the effectiveness with which the data is translated into something useful that a decision maker can utilise. The particular problem posed by large data volumes is twofold: first, the appropriate level of detail of the data needs to be identified and dealt with before presentation; second, data from disparate sources must be integrated to convey the full import of the underlying meaning that is contained in the organisation.

A practical manner to consider the issue of the quality of what is provided to the decision maker is offered by Dhar and Stein (1997). They use the term *Intelligence Density* to characterise the intelligence provided by a decision support tool. The concept of intelligence density accounts for the rate at which decision-specific information is generated for use by a decision maker. The proficiency with which useful information is generated is a function of automated and cognitive processes that make up decision making. Appropriate technologies and well-designed systems can do part of the work to provide useful information. The individual decision maker has to go the extra step to analytically process what is provided by the system in order to apply it to a decision-making task. The focus is on generating immediately useful and pertinent information and doing that in an efficient manner. By using appropriate technologies, some of the cognitive effort needed to produce pertinent information can be offloaded to a well-designed system. Broadly speaking, intelligence density is the ratio of the amount of useful information to the time taken to generate it. An organisation can increase its effectiveness and be more productive by increasing the intelligence density of the materials used by its decision makers. Some steps towards increasing the intelligence density of data used by decision makers is illustrated in Figure 7.1.

The process outlines a sequence of steps that converts potentially large amounts of raw data drawn from a variety of sources to highly pertinent and useful information chunks. In this chapter we want to examine some design-oriented methods that will enable us to realise this objective.

There are three relatively new technologies that can be used to address the issues that are outlined above. These technologies are capable of responding pointedly to the sequence outlined in Figure 7.1:

1. *Data Warehousing (DW)* which focuses on issues related to the capture and integrated management of large volumes of data.

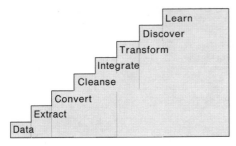

Figure 7.1. Steps for increasing intelligence density (from Dhar and Stein, 1997).

2. *On-Line Analytical Processing (OLAP)* which focuses on the analysis of large volumes of data in ways that directly address the decision-making needs of individuals.
3. *Data Mining (DM)* which seeks to automatically discover useful patterns of relationships that may be contained in the data.

These technologies are particularly relevant for the nature of the problems that we have addressed in this book. They have the potential of making a significant impact on the design and implementation of DSS applications. They are related to each other and it is therefore useful to consider them under a joint framework. Such a framework is presented in Figure 7.2. The framework serves as a useful guide for the architecture of a DSS application.

This framework seeks to highlight the complimentary nature of data warehouses, OLAP and data mining. The data warehouse and its related components extract, load, convert, scrub and transform the raw data available in the organisation into a form that allows the decision maker to effectively apply OLAP and data-mining tools. In the following sections we look at each one of these technologies in more detail and provide examples to illustrate their utility in decision making.

7.2 Data Warehousing

Data warehouses are at the heart of many information systems that rely heavily on data drawn from a variety of organisational processes and sources. They can therefore play a significant role in the design of decision support applications. The main function of a data warehouse is to provide data that is *integrated, subject-oriented, time-variant* and *non-volatile* to support managerial decision making (Inmon, 1992). We look at each of these important terms and their implications in more detail:

- *Subject-oriented* – the data warehouse is oriented towards the subjects that drive the organisation such as customers, vendors, products, etc. The data warehouse does not contain data that will not be used for decision support. This is an important distinction between data warehouses and the more traditional database-management systems.
- *Integrated* – the data found in a data warehouse is integrated, centralised and consolidated from data found scattered within and outside the organisation. The integration results in consistency in naming, measurement of variables, encoding structures, etc.
- *Time variant* – the contents of a data warehouse represents the flow of data through time. Data in the data warehouse is accurate at any moment of access and it typically

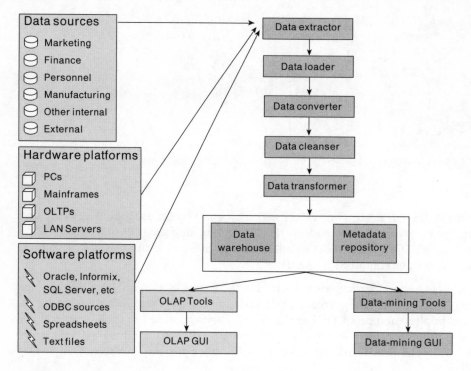

Figure 7.2. DSS Architecture incorporating Data Warehouses, OLAP, and Data Mining.

contains data that spans a long time horizon. Another implication of time variance is the inherent presence of time as a key component in the data structures of the data warehouse. Once the data in the data warehouse has been loaded, it is usually not updated.

- *Non-volatile* – once data enters the data warehouse, it is typically never removed (always growing). Unlike operational databases, there are no inserts, deletes or changes to the data stored in the data warehouse.

7.2.1 Process Issues in Data Warehousing

There are a number of steps that needs to be undertaken before data can enter a data warehouse or be analysed using OLAP or data-mining tools. Most data warehouses reside on relational platforms such as Oracle, Informix, Microsoft SQL Server, etc. As Figure 7.2 illustrates, the original or operational data from which the data warehouses are built can exist on a variety of hardware and software platforms. Apart from the varied platforms, operational data could also be extracted from a number of different sources from within and outside the organisation. This often requires the resolution of conflict-related issues (e.g. homonyms and synonyms) with respect to the data. The key steps that need to be undertaken to transform raw operational data to a form that can be stored in a data warehouse for analysis are:

- Extraction from a number of systems and loading the data into the data warehouse environment on a periodic basis.
- Converting the data into a common format appropriate to the data warehouse.
- Cleaning of the data so that there are no inconsistencies, inappropriate values, etc.

- Integration of the different datasets to suit the data model of the data warehouse.
- Transformation of the data through summarisation, aggregation, creation of new calculated attributes, etc.

Once these steps have been accomplished the data is ready for analysis. There are several options that can be utilised to carry out these steps: several specialised software environments may be employed to address the different steps in the process; alternatively, an integrated software platform capable of addressing most of the process may be employed. For example, Microsoft SQL Server 7 provides a Data Transformation Service (described in Section 7.2.5.1) by which raw data from operational data stores can be loaded, converted, cleansed, integrated and transformed.

7.2.2 Structure of the Data Warehouse

Data contained in a data warehouse can be broadly classified as belonging to three groups – metadata, data currency and data summarisation. In a sense, this could serve as an organising framework to view the data structure of a warehouse in its broadest form.

7.2.2.1 Metadata

Metadata consists of descriptions about users and data stored in the data warehouse. It is crucial to the building, functioning and management of the data warehouse because of its ability to make data comprehensible to the user. An important role of metadata is its ability to help the decision maker locate the contents of the data warehouse. Metadata typically contains:

- Names, definitions, structure, views and location of the data-warehouse objects.
- Integration, cleansing and transformation rules used to populate the data warehouse as well as the integration and transformation rules used to deliver the data to the decision maker.
- Authorisations, access control details, history of usage, ownership, etc.

7.2.2.2 Data Currency

Current detailed data is at the heart of the data warehouse. It reflects the data that is of immediate relevance to the decision-making process and is stored at the lowest level of granularity (highest level of detail). Current detailed data is stored according to a data model (schema or template) that describes the organisation of the data within the data warehouse, subject areas, relationships, keys, attributes and attribute groupings. The type of data model that is gaining a widespread following and acceptance is the *star schema* discussed in greater detail in Sections 7.2.3 and 7.2.5.2.

Older (dated) detailed data, as the name suggests, accumulates over time as fresh data enters the application. Its relevance may not be as immediate because of its lack of currency. However, the level of detail may be comparable with more current data based on its applicability to decision making. It is stored on mass storage media since its access is infrequent.

7.2.2.3 Data Summarisation

Data is lightly summarised and stored in the data warehouse. The data might be summarised over different units of time and different attributes. Data could also be found in a highly summarised form for quick retrieval. The highly summarised data could be physically stored within or outside the data warehouse but is logically considered a part of the data warehouse.

7.2.3 The Star Schema

A standard approach to considering the data model to support data-warehouse applications is the *star schema*. The data model must be capable of providing answers to complex queries that delve into different subject areas or dimensions of the organisation. The retrieval target is some collection of *facts* based on a specified set of *dimensions* or *subjects* (attributes). For example, a query such as "What is the sales amount of *Brand A Shampoos* in the third quarter of 1999 in all the WorldWideGrocer stores?" involves three dimensions or subjects: product (Brand A Shampoo), period (third quarter of 1999) and market (WorldWideGrocer). The retrieval has as a target one fact – sales. The star schema allows us to implement the data model that can answer such complex multidimensional queries using traditional relational platforms. This dimensional perspective on data is referred to as a cube (or a hypercube, depending on the number of dimensions). The idea is that each surface of the (hyper) cube is a particular dimension (or subject) of interest to the user with the relevant facts being the cube's contents. The star schema is a convenient way to show the relationships between the facts of interest and the relevant dimensions that need to be represented in the application. Using a relational approach for the implementation of this dimensional structure, the four key components of the star schema are:

- the fact table;
- dimension tables;
- attributes; and
- attribute hierarchies.

The fact table contains the facts (numeric values) that are relevant to the analysis. For example, in the query described above the fact sales would have to be stored in the fact table. The dimension tables contain details about the dimensions of relevance. In our example query reference is made to three dimension tables – product, period and market. Each dimension table contains a dimension value as an identifier. The dimension tables also contain attributes that allow us to search, filter and/or classify the facts contained in the fact table. Possible attributes for the product dimension table are brand, size, colour, etc. The time dimension may have the following as appropriate attributes – year, month, week, etc. These attributes can be ordered as a hierarchy allowing us to drill-down to greater levels of detail or roll-up to summaries. The fact table contains a primary key that is a concatenation of the primary keys of all the dimension tables. The term *multidimensional* is used frequently to refer to these applications where each dimension essentially refers to a particular perspective of the data.

7.2.4 Design Considerations

It should be clear by now that the emphasis with data-warehousing applications is on subject orientation and relevance to the decision-making situation. In designing a warehouse application, there are several important issues to consider in order to keep the subject orientation in perspective. Kimball (1996) makes some useful suggestions regarding a number of such issues to explicitly consider in the design of a data warehouse:

1. Identification of the fact tables by first identifying and studying the business processes

where data is being collected. The focus on the business process brings into sharp focus the relevant task-based perspectives on the data.

2. Deciding on various aspects about relevant facts such as:
   - the degree of detail of each fact (granularity);
   - identifying the dimensions of each fact table.
3. Deciding on various aspects about relevant dimensions such as:
   - deciding on the attributes of the dimensions;
   - identifying the process for tracking slowly changing dimensions.
4. The time duration of current detailed data – is it going to be 2 years or 5 or 10, etc.
5. The frequency with which the data from operational data stores are extracted, cleansed, transformed and loaded into the data warehouse.

7.2.5 Application Examples

In this section, we will discuss the application of the concepts that have been developed in this chapter. The examples are motivated by the retail-marketing application described in Chapter 4. It may be helpful at this stage to go over the details of this application with particular reference to the data aspects of that application. Recall that the application deals with promotion of specific products in retail outlets (markets). The type of data that we are interested in are sales volumes and promotion spending in different stores over time. The examples are developed in a representative software environment – the Microsoft SQL Server 7. There exist a number of alternative choices for the selection of an appropriate platform. We will first look at an example of the use of Data Transformation Services in Microsoft SQL Server 7 that allow us to extract and transform the raw operational data from a number of data sources into a form that could be loaded into the data warehouse. This is followed by another example that illustrates the actual creation of a data warehouse and its associated fact tables, dimension tables, etc.

7.2.5.1 Data Transformation Example

The examples in this section demonstrate the integration of data from an operational environment and its preparation in order to organise it within a data-warehouse environment. A database in the warehouse environment is first established. This is followed by the transformation of operational data into a form that is compatible with the warehouse using the Enterprise Manager environment of Microsoft SQL Server 7. This is accomplished with the use of a *data transformation package* using the palette illustrated in Figure 7.3. As shown in the figure, there are a few essential things that need to be specified to start the transformation process.

The sources of operational data must be appropriately declared. This aspect of the transformation is shown in the lower left corner of Figure 7.3. Typically, operational data comes from traditional data-management environments. However, Enterprise Manager allows the specified source to be a host of environments such as spreadsheets, ODBC sources, text files, etc. Furthermore, multiple sources of data may be declared as input into the warehouse. Figures 7.4a and 7.4b show two examples of declaring data sources. In the first case, operational data is provided from an Access database. In the second case, data is provided from three sources – an Access database, an Excel spreadsheet and an Informix database (an ODBC source).

Once the sources of data are defined, the next step is the precise definition of how the data is to be transformed before it is placed into the destination (the data warehouse). These transformation links can be specified in a variety of ways. The correspondence

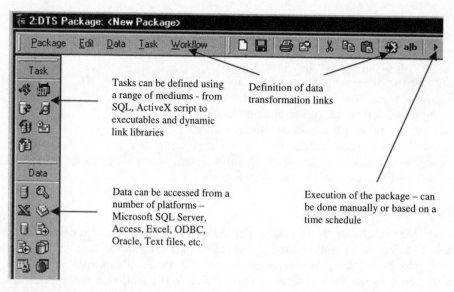

Figure 7.3. Data transformation palette.

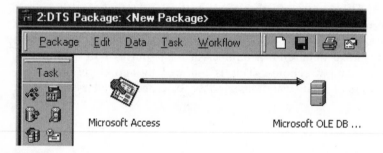

Figure 7.4a. Definition of the data transformation package – single data source.

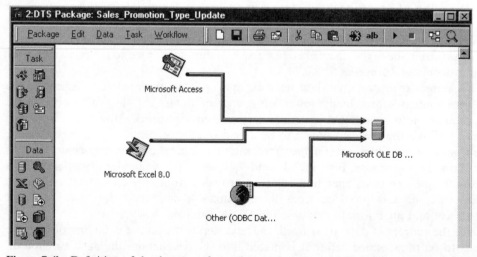

Figure 7.4b. Definition of the data transformation package – multiple data sources.

between the source labels and the destinations are first specified. This is typically followed by the use of one of several transformation link specifications:

- direct copying of a column from a source table to a destination table;
- transformation using a task script developed in a choice of languages;
- transformation using SQL queries that select data from the source based on specific selection criteria.

Figures 7.5a, 7.5b, and 7.5c show examples of how these might be accomplished in the Enterprise Manager environment offered by SQL Server.

The transformation process itself can be invoked on demand or can be scheduled to occur on a periodic basis – daily, weekly, monthly, etc.

7.2.5.2 Creation of the Star-Schema-based Data Warehouse

Apart from providing data transformation services, Enterprise Manager also provides facilities with which we can create new table structures and relationships between them. We continue with the retail marketing example in this section.

In the context of the retailing problem, the central facts that we are interested in relate to the sales of a particular product, in a particular market (or store), using a particular promotion, at a point in time. Hence, the fact table should contain facts related with sales such as sales quantity, the list price of the product, the standard cost of the product, level of promotion spending, etc. The obvious dimensions of this problem are the market, product, promotion and time. Figure 7.6 illustrates the creation of the dimension table market. Similarly we can create the other dimension tables and the fact table.

Once all the tables relevant to the star schema have been created, they can be linked into the star schema using a relationship/diagramming tool. A result of using this tool in the context of our problem is shown in Figure 7.7. Note that the primary key of the fact table is a compound key made up of the primary keys of all the dimension tables.

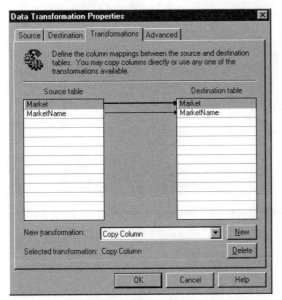

Figure 7.5a. Specification of the 'Copy Column' transformation process.

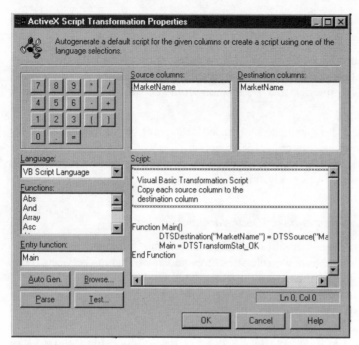

Figure 7.5b. Specification of transformation using ActiveX script in the link.

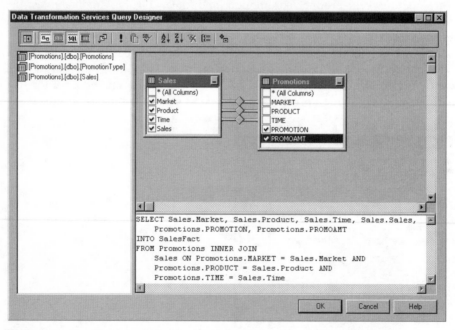

Figure 7.5c. Specification of the transformation through a visual query builder.

7.3 On-Line Analytical Processing (OLAP)

On-Line Analytical Processing can be broadly defined as creation, management, analysis and ad hoc querying of multidimensional data. Recall that multidimensional data refers to

	Column Name	Datatype	Length	Precision	Scale	Allow Nulls
⚷▶	Market	nvarchar	7	0	0	☐
	MarketName	nvarchar	50	0	0	✓
						☐

Figure 7.6. Specification of the market dimension table.

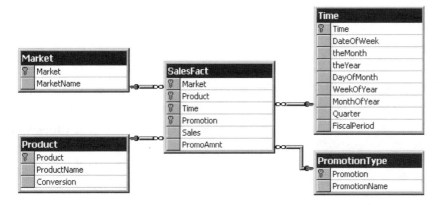

Figure 7.7. Star schema for the retailing application.

the multiple perspectives that users can have on the data depending on what the particular task is. The predominant focus of most OLAP systems are analysis and ad hoc querying of multidimensional data. The actual creation and management of multidimensional data is typically enabled using a data-warehousing system. On the face of it, it may appear that there are no significant differences between data-warehouses and OLAP systems. This might be due to the fact that they are complimentary technologies with a shared objective that is focused on the idea of improved intelligence density that we referred to earlier in this chapter. OLAP is a logical extension to a data warehouse. While the latter emphasises the provision of accurate, consistent, integrated and subject-wise data, the former leverages its availability for the purpose of enabling efficient analysis for decision making. Put another way, OLAP and related technologies focus on providing support for analytical modelling and computational requirements of decision makers while these processes are enabled by data-warehousing technology. OLAP systems also store their data in the form of the multidimensional data structures described earlier in the section on data warehouses. Hence, in this section we will look at the functional requirements of OLAP, structures or architectures of OLAP systems, representative sample of OLAP tools and examples of using the OLAP manager of Microsoft's SQL Server 7.

7.3.1 OLAP Functional Requirements

Some of the key requirements of OLAP systems include:

1. quick access to large amounts of data in a transparent manner;
2. ability to perform fast calculations;
3. ability to perform complex analysis;

4. powerful visualisation capabilities;
5. slice-and-dice data using various criteria;
6. drill-down to depths of detail (including the source relational databases if required) and roll-up to summaries;
7. ability to pivot or rearrange the orientation of dimensions of interest;
8. user-friendly interface.

In order for OLAP systems to work smoothly in conjunction with data warehouses, the ideas relating to multidimensional data mentioned earlier must flow seamlessly between the two. In particular, support must be provided for the ability to specify an application using dimensionally oriented designs (e.g. the star schema), the idea of data cubes in the use of the dimensions and having an arbitrary number of dimensions in an application. Typically, these applications are deployed in environments involving multiple users working in a client–server environment.

7.3.2 Structure of OLAP systems

Several alternative approaches to deploying OLAP systems in a client–server environment exist. Regardless of the particular approach taken, there are a few basic essential components that are necessary to successfully implement OLAP applications. We briefly discuss what they are.

- *Data store* – detailed data, metadata and summarised data – can be stored in a data warehouse that resides on a central server, or some of the data (slice of the data warehouse) could also be redundantly made available on the client.
- *Data-management system* – RDBMS or proprietary multidimensional database management system – could reside on the server (advisable) or could be on the client (need a powerful client) or it can be in a middle tier of the client–server architecture.
- *Analysis engine to accomplish bulk multidimensional calculations* – generally accomplished on the server but as above can be located on a middle tier or even on the client (provided the client is powerful enough).
- *Analysis engine to accomplish ad-hoc multidimensional calculations* – usually found on the middle tier if one exists or on the client.
- *A Graphical User Interface (GUI)* – mostly found on the client but with the advent of relatively newer technologies – such as the Microsoft Terminal Server, Citrix, etc. – the GUI can be located on the server or middle tier and can be accessed through a program such as the Terminal Server Client or Citrix client.

An important aspect in the context of the architecture of OLAP systems is the storage of multidimensional data. Three of the more common variations for the structure are:

- multidimensional OLAP (MOLAP);
- relational OLAP (ROLAP);
- hybrid OLAP (HOLAP).

MOLAP, as the name implies, uses a multidimensional data-storage format and gives the best performance for multidimensional data queries. MOLAP storage is appropriate for small to medium-sized databases. Both the detailed data as well as the aggregations and summaries are stored in the MOLAP server.

With the ROLAP storage architecture the data is stored in their original relational storage structures. Aggregations and summaries are stored in separate relational tables. The ROLAP architecture is appropriate when the database size is medium to large.

Hybrid OLAP or HOLAP tries to take advantage of the strengths of MOLAP and OLAP. It maintains the original detailed data in their relational data-storage formats but keeps aggregations in the multidimensional data-storage format. This allows the architecture to access huge databases and, at the same time, have very fast query access to aggregations.

7.3.3 Tools

With data being the heart of OLAP applications, most of the database vendors have entered the OLAP market by providing OLAP tools that integrate well with their DBMS. Oracle's Express, Microsoft SQL Server 7's OLAP services, Red Brick Warehouse's OLAP extensions to SQL, etc. are all examples of this trend. Apart from these products, other major players in the OLAP tools market are Cognos with PowerPlay, Information Builder's Inc's FOCUS Fusion, Pilot Software's Pilot Decision Support Suite, Brio Technology Inc.'s BrioQuery, etc.

7.3.4 Examples

In this section we will first look at an example of the use of the Cube Wizard in the OLAP Manager of Microsoft SQL Server 7 that allows us to specify the multidimensional data structure from the fact table(s) with the facts tied to the dimension tables and their attributes. This is followed by another example that illustrates the use of the Storage Design Wizard to specify whether the architecture is going to be MOLAP, ROLAP or a HOLAP. Finally, we show some examples of using the OLAP system by slicing, dicing, pivoting, drilling-down and rolling-up of the multidimensional data.

7.3.4.1 OLAP Server Creation Example

In the examples from the data-warehousing section we created the star schema within the SQL Server 7 environment. In this example, we create the star schema using the OLAP Manager that is an add-on to SQL Server 7. As in the case of the data-warehouse example, here too we need to start by creating a database to store the OLAP server. Following this we specify the data sources that feed into the OLAP server (Figure 7.8).

Once all the required data sources have been specified we use the cube wizard to define the dimensional data model/star schema. The specifications that need to be provided at this stage are:

- details about the fact table and its contents;
- dimensions that are relevant to the application;
- selection of a storage structure for the data (MOLAP, ROLAP, or HOLAP).

In our application, the fact table must contain data that relates to sales. Specifically, these are the sales amount, the amount spent on promotion, the product list price and the product standard cost. These are specified as the relevant attributes of the fact table and are referred to as the 'cube measures'. This means that they will be the target of retrievals motivated by the specification of particular dimensions. Figures 7.9a and 7.9b show the set up of the fact table and the nomination of the cube measures.

The relevant dimensions in our application are:

- *Time* – this allows us to examine the data using time-based criteria such as weekly or monthly sales (or promotion spending).

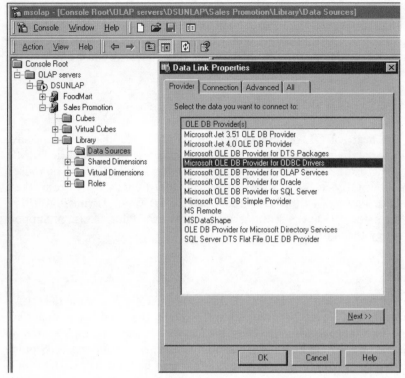

Figure 7.8. Definition of the data source for the OLAP server.

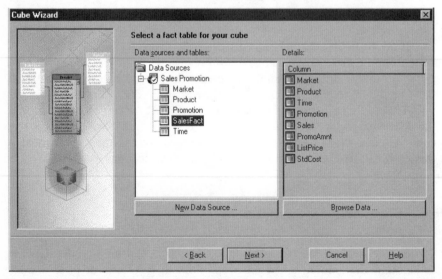

Figure 7.9a. Specifying the fact table from the data source.

- *Market* – this enables us to examine the data by a particular market (e.g. sales amount in each of the selected markets).
- *Promotion* – this allows us to examine sales by a particular promotion type (e.g. sales amount for the coupon promotion type).
- *Product* – allows us to examine sales, promotion spending, etc. by product.

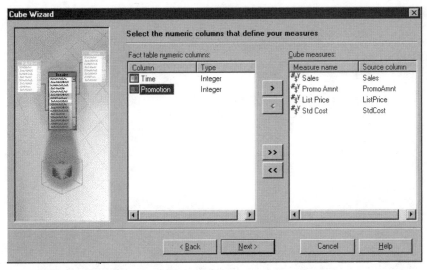

Figure 7.9b. Specification of the facts (cube measures).

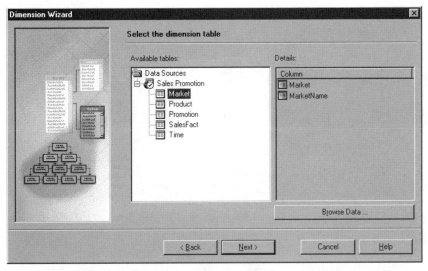

Figure 7.10a. Selecting the market dimension table.

Each of these dimensions is specified and linked to the fact table using the star schema. To illustrate the process, we take the market dimension and show its definition in Figures 7.10a and 7.10b. The final star schema that results from defining all the dimensions mentioned above is shown in Figure 7.10c.

7.3.4.2 OLAP Server Storage Design Example

The Storage Design Wizard allows the user to select the type of storage that is appropriate – MOLAP, ROLAP or HOLAP (Figure 7.11). It also allows the setting of aggregation options (Figure 7.12). As the number of aggregations increases, the space required to store them also increases. At the same time, the speed of answering queries

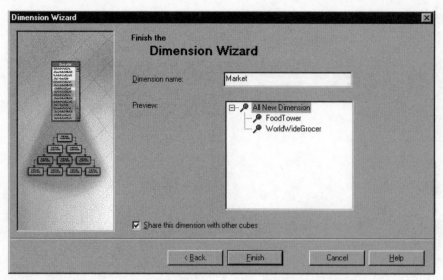

Figure 7.10b. Naming the market dimension and previewing its information.

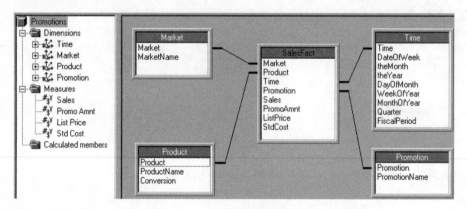

Figure 7.10c. View of completed star schema for the retailing application.

increases as well. The user has the option of selecting either a space-constrained approach or performance-oriented approach. Alternatively, the user may specify the appropriate aggregation level manually.

7.3.4.3 OLAP Server Usage (Slice and Dice, Pivot, Drill-Down and Roll-up) Examples

Once the cubes and data storage have been specified, as shown in the examples above, the decision maker can start using the OLAP server. Multidimensional access to the data can be facilitated through the use of the cube browser. In the following examples we explore just a few of the operations possible on the data. Figures 7.13–7.16 illustrate different views of the multidimensional data through slicing and dicing.

Figure 7.17a allows the decision maker to view all the relevant facts for all markets aggregated by product, promotion and time. Note that there is a '+' sign besides the year column indicating that we can drill-down to greater depths of detail if required.

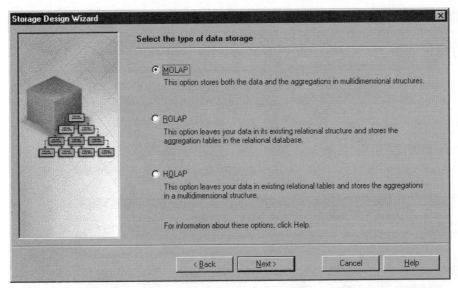

Figure 7.11. Specification of the type of data storage – MOLAP, ROLAP or HOLAP.

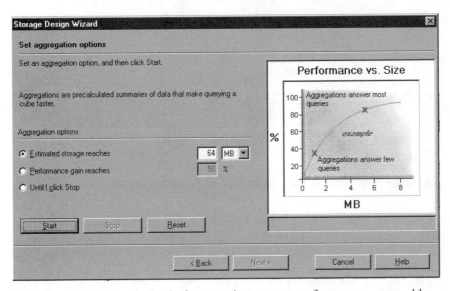

Figure 7.12. Setting up the level of aggregation – space, performance or manual base.

Also note that a pivoting operation has been done on the measures, what was a columnar attribute has now become a row attribute.

Drilling-down on the year column in Figure 7.17a results in Figure 7.17b allowing us to view details by week. Note that there is now a '–' sign besides the year column indicating that we can roll-up to summaries if required.

7.4 Data Mining

Data mining can be defined as the process of identifying valid, novel, useful and understandable patterns in data through automatic or semi-automatic means. Data

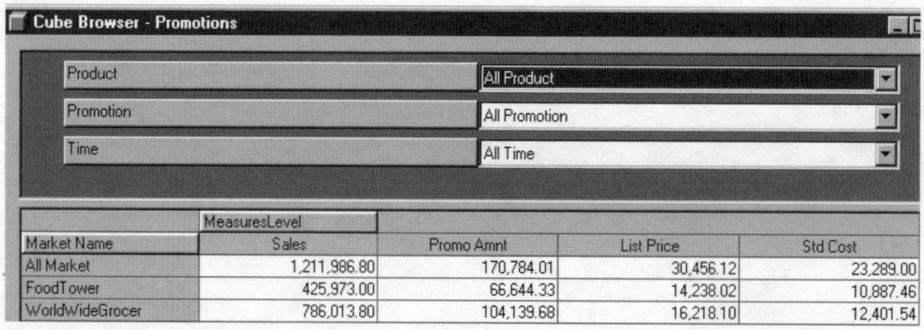

	MeasuresLevel			
Market Name	Sales	Promo Amnt	List Price	Std Cost
All Market	1,211,986.80	170,784.01	30,456.12	23,289.00
FoodTower	425,973.00	66,644.33	14,238.02	10,887.46
WorldWideGrocer	786,013.80	104,139.68	16,218.10	12,401.54

Figure 7.13. Viewing all facts for all markets aggregated by product, promotion and time.

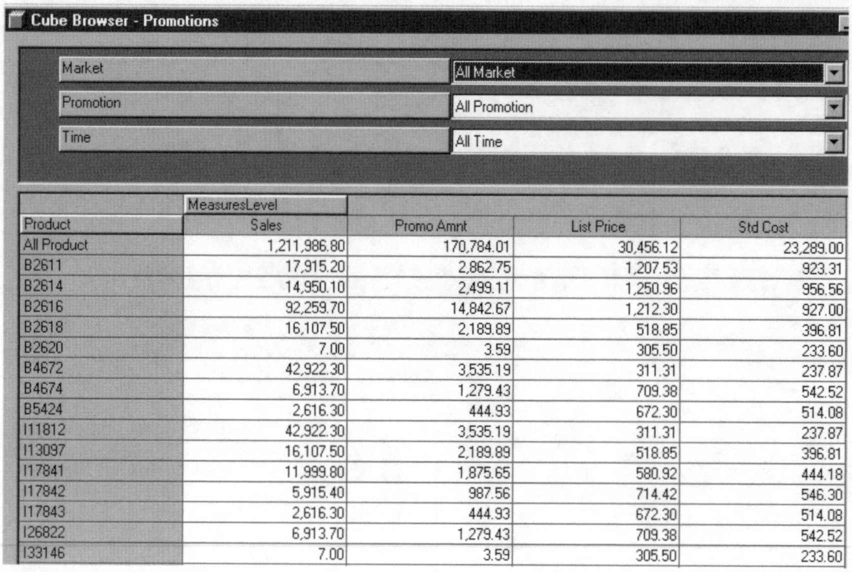

	MeasuresLevel			
Product	Sales	Promo Amnt	List Price	Std Cost
All Product	1,211,986.80	170,784.01	30,456.12	23,289.00
B2611	17,915.20	2,862.75	1,207.53	923.31
B2614	14,950.10	2,499.11	1,250.96	956.56
B2616	92,259.70	14,842.67	1,212.30	927.00
B2618	16,107.50	2,189.89	518.85	396.81
B2620	7.00	3.59	305.50	233.60
B4672	42,922.30	3,535.19	311.31	237.87
B4674	6,913.70	1,279.43	709.38	542.52
B5424	2,616.30	444.93	672.30	514.08
I11812	42,922.30	3,535.19	311.31	237.87
I13097	16,107.50	2,189.89	518.85	396.81
I17841	11,999.80	1,875.65	580.92	444.18
I17842	5,915.40	987.56	714.42	546.30
I17843	2,616.30	444.93	672.30	514.08
I26822	6,913.70	1,279.43	709.38	542.52
I33146	7.00	3.59	305.50	233.60

Figure 7.14. Viewing all facts for all markets aggregated by product, promotion and time.

mining uses techniques that originated from diverse fields such as computer science, statistics, artificial intelligence, etc. Data mining is now being used in a range of industries and for a range of tasks. In this section we first look at a classification of data mining, then at the process of data mining, some prominent data-mining tools and finally examples of using one of the tools.

7.4.1 Classification of Data Mining

The complexity of the field of data mining makes it worthwhile to structure the goals, tasks, methods, algorithms and algorithm implementations of data mining in an hierarchical form as illustrated in Figure 7.18 (Kingan, 1998).

The goals of data mining drive the tasks that need to be undertaken, and the tasks drive the methods that will be applied. The methods that will be applied determine the selections of specific algorithms followed by the choice of algorithm implementations.

The goals of data mining can be description, prediction and/or verification. Description involves fitting a model to a set of data trying to establish an explanation of the data and to present patterns to decision makers in an understandable form.

Figure 7.15. Viewing all facts for all products and promotions aggregated by market and time.

Figure 7.16. Viewing all facts for all products and the temporary price reduction promotion aggregated by market and time.

Prediction involves using the model developed through description to predict the future. Quite often prediction and description have been clubbed together and referred to as discovery. Verification involves the proposal and verification of the decision maker's hypothesis.

The tasks that need to be undertaken to support the goals of data mining can vary, ranging from prediction-oriented tasks like classification and regression to

	Cube Browser - Promotions				□

Product		All Product		▼
Promotion		All Promotion		▼

		Market Name		
+ Year	MeasuresLevel	All Market	FoodTower	WorldWideGrocer
All Time	Sales	1,211,986.80	425,973.00	786,013.80
	Promo Amnt	170,784.01	66,644.33	104,139.68
	List Price	30,456.12	14,238.02	16,218.10
	Std Cost	23,289.00	10,887.46	12,401.54
+ 1992	Sales	1,211,986.80	425,973.00	786,013.80
	Promo Amnt	170,784.01	66,644.33	104,139.68
	List Price	30,456.12	14,238.02	16,218.10
	Std Cost	23,289.00	10,887.46	12,401.54

Figure 7.17a. Viewing all the relevant facts for all markets aggregated by product, promotion and time and drilling-down on the time dimension.

	Cube Browser - Promotions			

Product		All Product		▼
Promotion		All Promotion		▼

			Market Name		
- Year	Week	MeasuresLevel	All Market	FoodTower	WorldWideGrocer
- 1992	Week 6	Sales	43,479.00	17,700.00	25,779.00
		Promo Amnt	8,628.42	3,723.83	4,904.59
		List Price	1,320.43	478.70	841.73
		Std Cost	1,009.67	366.04	643.63
	Week 7	Sales	49,479.00	18,888.00	30,591.00
		Promo Amnt	8,142.56	3,290.58	4,851.98
		List Price	1,323.29	476.98	846.31
		Std Cost	1,011.85	364.70	647.15
	Week 8	Sales	47,633.00	19,464.00	28,169.00
		Promo Amnt	8,030.54	3,539.22	4,491.32
		List Price	1,437.02	598.36	838.66
		Std Cost	1,098.82	457.52	641.30
	Week 9	Sales	46,770.00	16,452.00	30,318.00
		Promo Amnt	6,406.60	2,473.09	3,933.51
		List Price	1,252.68	479.70	772.98

Figure 7.17b. Viewing all the relevant facts for all markets in different weeks and aggregated by product and promotion and allowing rolling-up on the time dimension.

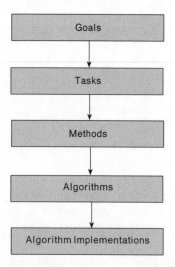

Figure 7.18. Hierarchy of data mining (from Kingan, 1998).

description-oriented tasks like clustering, summarisation, deviation detection and visualisation and verification-oriented statistical-analysis techniques.

Methods or techniques to carry out these tasks are many, chief among them are:

- neural networks;
- rule induction;
- market basket analysis;
- cluster detection;
- link analysis;
- statistical analysis.

Each method may have several supporting algorithms and in turn each algorithm may be implemented in a different manner.

7.4.2 Process of Data Mining

Data mining can be thought of as part of a larger process – knowledge discovery in databases (KDD) (Fayyad *et al.*, 1996) (Figure 7.19). In terms of increasing the intelligence density in an organisation, this process has a lot in common with data warehousing and OLAP processes. The process is by necessity interactive and iterative in nature. The first step involves understanding the application domain, goals of the decision maker and, based on that, selecting a subset of the enterprise data for knowledge discovery. The second step is pre-processing, where data are cleaned, issues related with missing values, unknown values, noise and outliers dealt with. The third step involves transforming the data into a form that is appropriate for data mining – data reduction and projection. The fourth step involves choosing the function of data mining (classification,

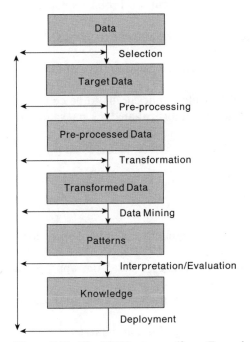

Figure 7.19. The KDD process (from Fayyad *et al.*, 1996).

summarisation, clustering, regression, etc), choosing the specific algorithm to carry out the function and finally conduct the data-mining exercise through the search for patterns. The fifth step involves the interpretation and evaluation of the pattern and translating the knowledge into a form that is understandable to decision makers so that they can take actions based upon it. The process of selection, pre-processing and transformation will not be required if data mining is conducted on data warehouses since the data that enters the data warehouse have already been selected, pre-processed and transformed.

As mentioned earlier, the two key data-mining goals are verification (hypothesis testing) and discovery (description and prediction). Another way to think of discovery is directed knowledge discovery and undirected knowledge discovery (Berry and Linoff, 1997). In directed knowledge discovery the purpose is to explain the value of certain variables (dependent) in terms of others (independent); that is, the decision maker specifies the dependent and independent variables. In undirected knowledge discovery the decision maker does not specify the dependent or target variable. The system is asked to identify patterns that may be novel, valid or significant. In known domains the decision maker might use directed knowledge discovery but in unfamiliar domains the decision maker might use undirected knowledge discovery to recognise relationships among variables first and then use directed knowledge discovery to explain those relationships.

Though the KDD process described above is valid and useful, it is worthwhile to look at the processes suggested by Berry and Linoff (1997) specifically in the context of hypothesis testing, directed knowledge discovery and undirected knowledge discovery as listed in the following sections.

7.4.3 Hypothesis Testing

The main steps in hypothesis testing are:

1. Generate hypotheses through identification and statement of problems facilitated through interviews with organisational decision makers.
2. Determine/define the data that would be needed to test the above hypotheses.
3. Locate the data identified in the previous step.
4. Prepare the data for analysis – the pre-processing and transformation steps of the KDD process.
5. Build computer models based on the data – the mental model needs to be converted into a computer model that can be implemented on statistical-analysis packages like SAS or SPSS.
6. Apply the computer model and evaluate it to confirm or reject the hypotheses.

7.4.4 Directed Knowledge Discovery

The main steps in directed knowledge discovery are:

1. Identify the sources of pre-classified data like data warehouses (preferable), operational data sources and/or external data sources.
2. Prepare the data for analysis – deciding on the amount of data, the appropriate variables and segregating training, testing and evaluation datasets.
3. Build and train the computer model using methods that are appropriate to the data-mining technique being used.
4. Evaluate the computer model against the pre-classified evaluation dataset.
5. Apply the computer model to new datasets.

7.4.5 Undirected Knowledge Discovery

In undirected knowledge discovery we conduct all the steps listed above as part of the directed knowledge discovery process as well as the two steps listed below:

1. Identify potential targets for directed knowledge discovery.
2. Generate new hypotheses to test.

7.4.6 Tools

There are a number of data-mining tools that support the goals, tasks, methods and algorithms that we listed earlier. Westphal and Blaxton (1998) describe in detail some of the prominent data mining tools and classify them in three categories:

- Quantitative data-mining tools like Clementine, Enterprise Miner, Diamond, Cross-Graphs, etc.
- Landscape-visualisation tools like MineSet, Metaphor Mixer, AVS/Express, IBM Visualization Data Explorer, Visible Decisions in 3D, etc.
- Link analysis tools like NETMAP, Analyst's Notebook, Daisy, Imagix 4D, Crime Link, etc.

7.4.7 Examples

Amongst the different data-mining techniques, some can be perceived as being passive where the decision maker needs to interpret the results, while some can be perceived as being active where the system itself finds the features/patterns underlying the data. In a previous chapter we looked at the use of Clementine in the context of visualisation and we saw examples of the use of histograms, network models (web), charts and classification models. Apart from the classification model, the rest of the examples dealt with passive data-mining techniques. But in the following examples we look at the use of Clementine in the context of active data-mining techniques like neural networks, rule induction, kohonen networks and generalised rule induction (GRI). We use the United States Census Bureau dataset that we introduced in Chapter 6 to drive these examples. Before we look at the examples we first look at the components of Clementine and the way they support the KDD process.

7.4.7.1 Clementine Support for the KDD Process

Clementine supports the entire KDD process by providing various features (Figure 7.20). First and foremost it supports the selection of data by allowing the decision maker to link to a number of data sources through variable and fixed file formats as well as ODBC. It also supports the data pre-processing and data-transformation steps of the KDD process by providing various record and field-operation features. The graphing features allow passive data mining while the modelling features support active data mining. Finally, the output features support the evaluation of the models. Apart from evaluation, the output features also support various statistical-analysis tools that help in hypothesis testing.

7.4.7.2 Neural Networks

The basic unit of a neural network is a neuron. Neurons are arranged in the form of layers. There are three key layers – the input layer, the hidden layer(s) and the output layer. Data

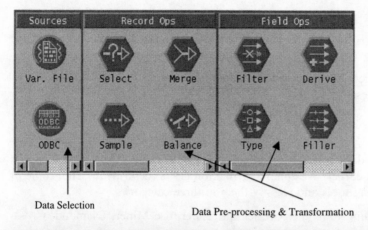

Data Selection

Data Pre-processing & Transformation

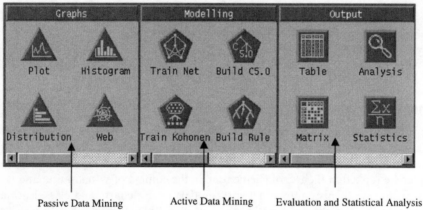

Passive Data Mining   Active Data Mining   Evaluation and Statistical Analysis

Figure 7.20. Clementine support for the KDD process.

is presented to the input layer and the value is propagated to every neuron in the next layer till the result is obtained from the output layer. The values change as they propagate through the network through the use of weights. As the network processes data it learns and modifies the weights; that is, it gets trained such that it is able to accurately replicate the results. After training, the neural network can be applied to cases where the result is not known for prediction. While neural networks are accurate and capable of modelling complex relationships they lack explainability and are difficult to interpret.

In the following example we train a neural network to predict whether a person will have a salary greater than £20,000, or less than or equal to £20,000, based on the independent variables age, number of years of education, sex, capital gains and number of hours worked per week. The Clementine stream to accomplish this, as well as analyse the effectiveness of the neural network, is illustrated in Figure 7.21a. There is a default novice mode for specifying the neural network, as illustrated in Figure 21b, as well as an expert mode, as illustrated in Figure 7.21c. The results of training the network indicates the number of neurons in the different layers, the predicted accuracy of the model, as well as the relative importance of the independent variables (Figure 7.21d). The stream also produces an analysis of the effectiveness of the neural network as illustrated in Figure 7.21e. This has various measures for the accuracy of the results produced by the neural network.

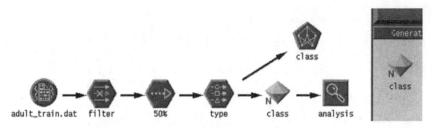

Figure 7.21a. Using a neural network for predicting salary.

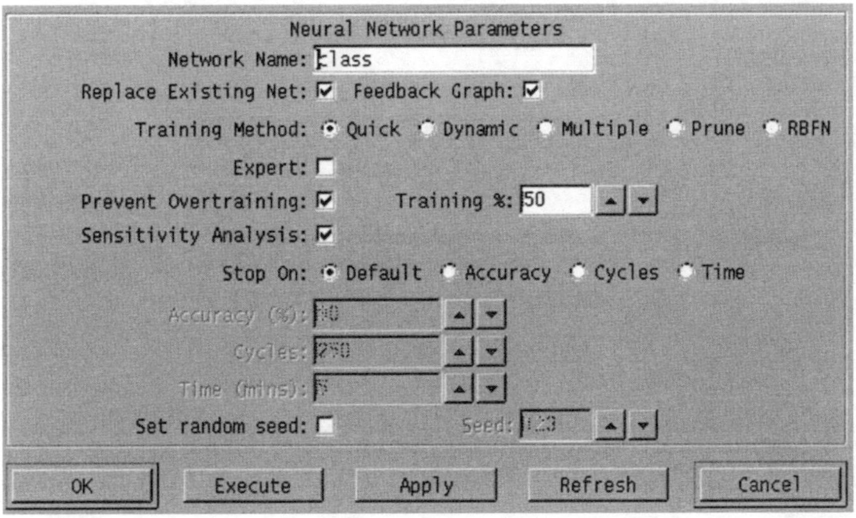

Figure 7.21b. Specifying the behaviour of the neural network using the novice mode.

7.4.7.3 Rule Induction

Rule induction builds models that are easy to understand and are of the form:

IF *condition* THEN *action*

An example of this is as follows:

IF *education level is high* THEN *salary* $> £20,000$

Rule induction creates a decision tree representing the rules for classifying data into different results/outcomes. The advantage of the decision-tree approach is that only important factors are considered. These decision trees are then converted into the above mentioned IF–THEN rulesets. Unlike the opaqueness of neural networks the rules created through induction produce a model that is understandable and close to the way humans think.

In the following example we apply the C5.0 Rule Induction algorithm to create a ruleset that would help us in predicting whether a person will have a salary greater than £20,000, or less than or equal to £20,000, based on the independent variables age, number of years of education, sex, capital gains, and number of hours worked per week. The Clementine stream to accomplish this as well as analyse the effectiveness of the

```
                        Neural Network Parameters
              Network Name: class
        Replace Existing Net: ☑  Feedback Graph: ☑

             Training Method: ⦿ Quick  ○ Dynamic  ○ Multiple  ○ Prune  ○ RBFN

                      Expert: ☑
        Prevent Overtraining: ☑      Training %: 50     ▲ ▼
        Sensitivity Analysis: ☑

                     Stop On: ⦿ Default  ○ Accuracy  ○ Cycles  ○ Time
               Accuracy (%):            ▲ ▼
                     Cycles:            ▲ ▼
                Time (mins):            ▲ ▼
             Set random seed: ☐           Seed:        ▲ ▼
```
```
                         Quick Expert Options
        Hidden Layers: ⦿ One  ○ Two  ○ Three

        Layer 1: 20    ▲ ▼  2:       ▲ ▼  3:       ▲ ▼
        Persistence: 200   ▲ ▼
```
```
                            Learning Rates
        Alpha: 0.9      ▲ ▼

        Initial Eta: 0.3    ▲ ▼ Eta Decay: 30    ▲ ▼

        High Eta: 0.1   ▲ ▼ Low Eta: 0.01   ▲ ▼
```
```
        [   OK   ]    [ Execute ]    [  Apply  ]    [ Refresh ]    [ Cancel ]
```

Figure 7.21c. Specifying the behaviour of the neural network using the expert mode.

```
Neural Network "class" architecture

Input Layer     : 5 neurons
Hidden Layer #1 : 4 neurons
Output Layer    : 1 neurons

Predicted Accuracy :  82.12%

Relative Importance of Inputs
capital-gain          : 0.68775
education-num         : 0.46533
age                   : 0.35955
hours-per-week        : 0.29171
sex                   : 0.12978
```

Figure 7.21d. Architecture of the neural network model.

```
Results for output field class
    Comparing $N-class with class
        Correct    :     4105    ( 82.10%)
        Wrong      :      895    ( 17.90%)
        Total      :     5000
        Confidence Values Report for $NC-class
            Range                  : 0.0004 - 0.9950
            Mean Correct           : 0.6738
            Mean Incorrect         : 0.3578
            Always Correct Above   : 0.9898 ( 5.6% of cases)
            Always Incorrect Below : 0.0008 ( 0.0% of cases)
            90.0% accuracy above    : 0.3585
            2.0 fold correct above  : 0.3980 (91.1% accuracy)
```

Figure 7.21e. Analysis results of the neural network model.

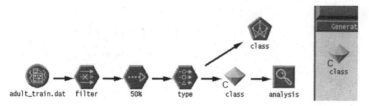

Figure 7.22a. Using a C5.0 Rule Induction algorithm for predicting salary.

C5.0 Induction Parameters

Output name: class

Mode: ⦿ Build Model ○ Cross-validate [   ] ▲ ▼ fold

Output type: ⦿ Decision Tree ○ Ruleset

Group symbolic values: ☐

Use Boosting: ☐ Number of trials: [   ] ▲ ▼

Method: ⦿ Simple ○ Expert

Simple Options

Favour: ⦿ Accuracy ○ Generality

Expected noise (%): 0   0 [▭] _____ 50

| OK | Execute | Apply | Refresh | Cancel |

Figure 7.22b. Specifying the behaviour of the C5.0 Rule Induction algorithm using the novice mode.

ruleset/model created by the C5.0 algorithm is illustrated in Figure 7.22a. There is a default novice mode for specifying the C5.0 Rule Induction parameters, as illustrated in Figure 7.22b, as well as an expert mode, as illustrated in Figure 7.22c. The execution of the stream could result in a decision tree (Figure 7.22d) or in a ruleset (Figure 7.22e) depending on the parameter set. The stream also produces an analysis of the effectiveness of the C5.0 ruleset as illustrated in Figure 7.22f. This has various measures for the accuracy of the results produced by the C5.0 ruleset.

7.4.7.4 Generalised Rule Induction (GRI)

Generalised Rule Induction (GRI) is a means of coming up with association rules which specify conclusions for a set of conditions. GRI finds associations that would have been possible through a visual inspection of a network model (web). The key difference to the C5.0 type of decision-tree algorithm is that GRI can associate any attribute and the rules generated through GRI can have many conclusions. Rules are first generated and then tested against the data. Good rules are kept and others pruned. Starting from simple rules more complex conditions are added and a similar process of test and prune is conducted till a set of good rules are produced. This set of rules cannot be directly used for prediction because of the many conclusions possible and requires refinement. Refinement can be used to produce a ruleset that can then be used for prediction.

The stream in Figure 7.23a illustrates a stream that produces an unrefined GRI model which is then refined to produce a ruleset that is then analysed for accuracy. Figures 7.23b and 7.23c illustrate screens that allow the decision maker to define the parameters for the execution of the GRI algorithm. Figure 7.23d is the result of the unrefined GRI

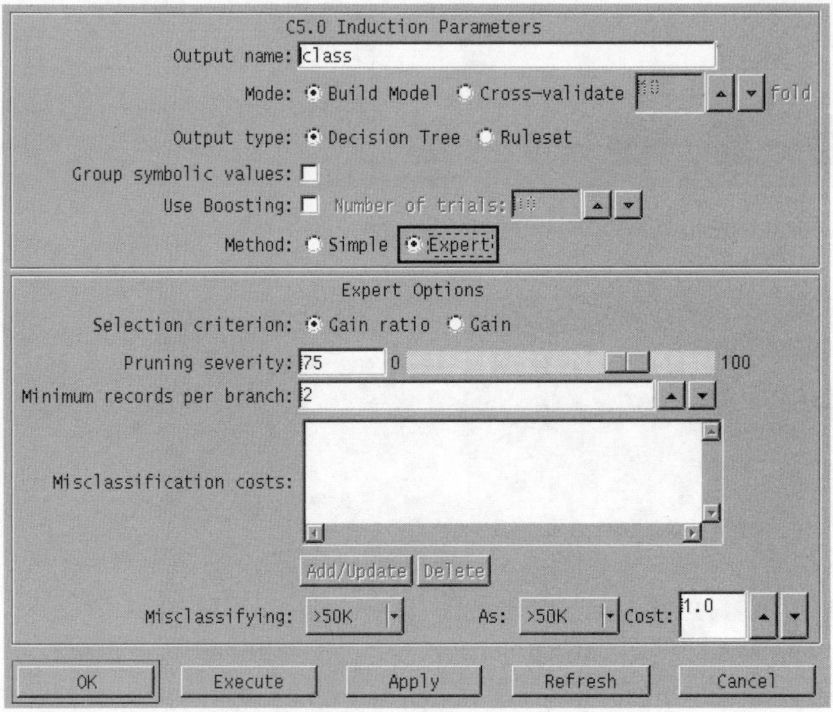

Figure 7.22c. Specifying the behaviour of the C5.0 Rule Induction algorithm using the expert mode.

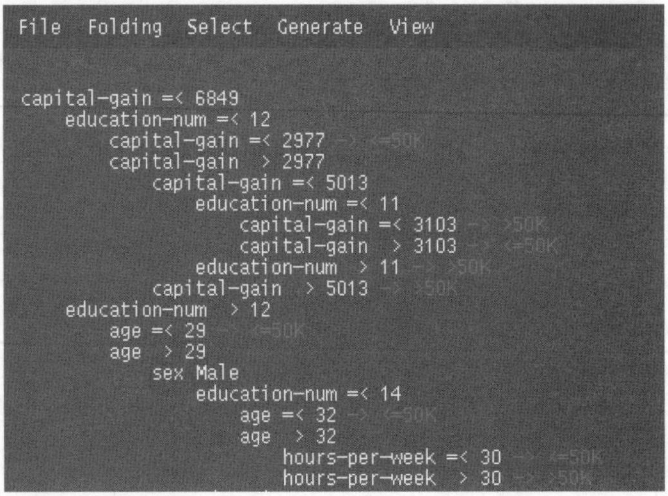

Figure 7.22d. Decision tree created by the C5.0 Rule Induction algorithm.

model. When this is refined it results in a ruleset, as illustrated in Figure 7.23e. Results of applying the refined ruleset are illustrated in Figure 7.23f.

7.5 Conclusion

In this chapter we have looked at three emergent technologies that have and will continue to have a significant impact on the design and implementation of DSS. In the introduction

```
File   Folding   Select   Generate   View

Rules for    50K :
    Rule #1 for   50K :
        if   capital-gain > 5013
        then      50K

    Rule #2 for   50K :
        if   age > 29
        and   education-num > 14
        and   sex == Male
        and   hours-per-week <= 30
        then      50K

    Rule #3 for   50K :
        if   age > 29
        and   education-num > 12
        and   sex == Female
        and   hours-per-week > 62
        and   hours-per-week <= 66
        then      50K
```

Figure 7.22e. Ruleset created by the C5.0 Rule Induction algorithm.

```
File


Results for output field class
    Comparing $C-class with class
        Correct   :      4167    ( 83.34%)
        Wrong     :       833    ( 16.66%)
        Total     :      5000
        Confidence Values Report for $CC-class
            Range                    : 0.5829 - 1.0000
            Mean Correct             : 0.8431
            Mean Incorrect           : 0.7813
            Always Correct Above     : 1.0000 ( 0.2% of cases)
            Always Incorrect Below   : 0.5829 ( 2.1% of cases)
            90.0% accuracy above     : 0.8627
            2.0 fold correct above   : 0.8627 (91.7% accuracy)
```

Figure 7.22f. Analysis results of using the C5.0 ruleset.

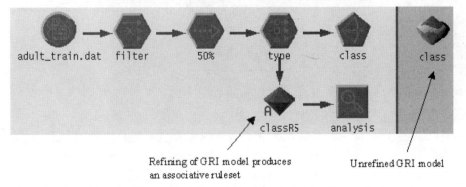

Refining of GRI model produces
an associative ruleset

Unrefined GRI model

Figure 7.23a. Using the Generalised Rule Induction algorithm for predicting salary.

to this chapter (Section 7.1) we introduced a DSS architecture that complementarily uses data warehousing, OLAP and data mining. In Section 7.2 we studied data warehousing, the processes involved in it, their structure, the steps involved in building a data warehouse, tools used in building one and finally examples of constructing and using a

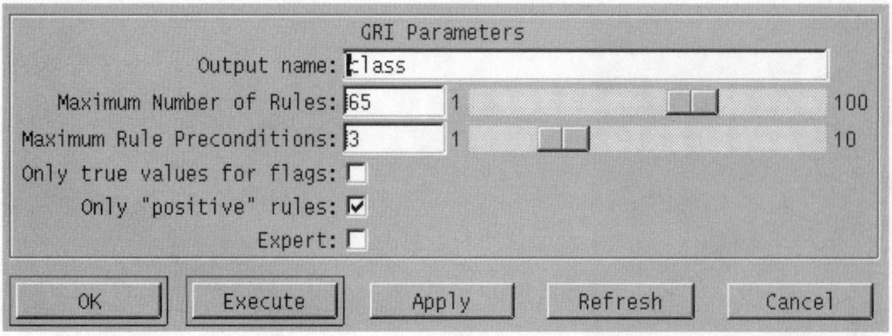

Figure 7.23b. Specifying the behaviour of the GRI algorithm using the novice mode.

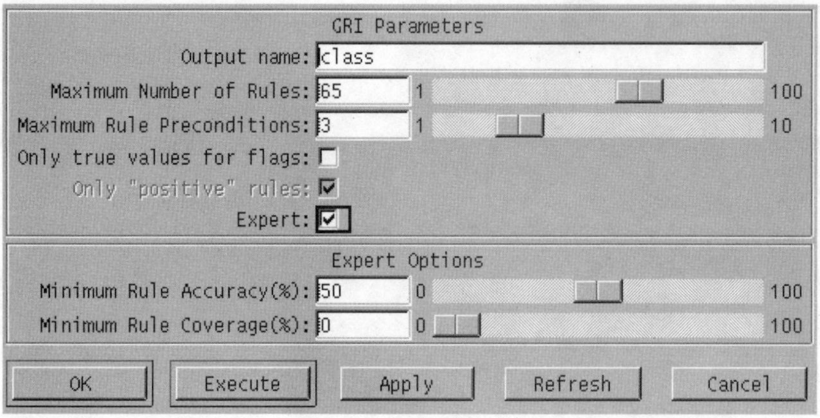

Figure 7.23c. Specifying the behaviour of the GRI algorithm using the expert mode.

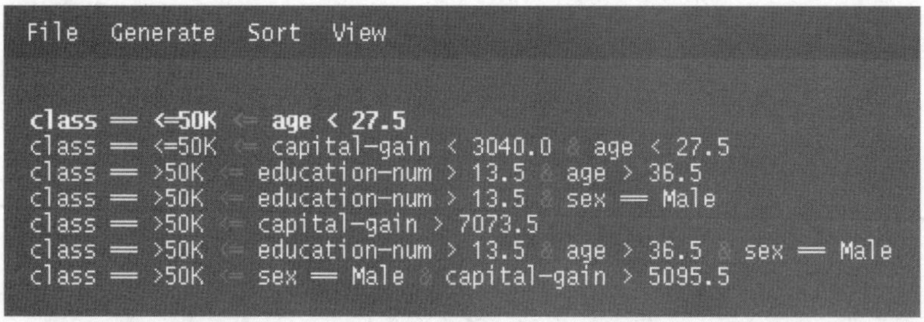

Figure 7.23d. Unrefined associative rules created using the Generalised Rule Induction algorithm.

data warehouse. Section 7.2 also introduced a very important multidimensional data model – the star schema – that has implications for data warehousing as well as OLAP. Section 7.3 introduced OLAP, its functional requirements, structure, tools and finally examples of creating and using an OLAP system. Section 7.4 introduced data mining and a classification of the same, the processes involved in data mining in general and more specifically in hypothesis testing, directed and undirected knowledge discovery, tools of data mining and finally examples of using a data-mining system.

```
File   Folding   Select   Generate   View


Rules for <=50K:
    Rule #1 for <=50K:
        if  capital-gain < 4243.5
        and  age < 29.5
        then -> <=50K

    Rule #2 for <=50K:
        if  age < 27.5
        then -> <=50K

Rules for >50K:
    Rule #1 for >50K:
        if  capital-gain > 7073.5
        then -> >50K

    Rule #2 for >50K:
        if  sex == Male
        and  capital-gain > 5095.5
        then -> >50K

    Rule #3 for >50K:
        if  education-num > 13.5
        and  sex == Male
        then -> >50K

    Rule #4 for >50K:
        if  education-num > 13.5
        and  age > 36.5
        and  sex == Male
        then -> >50K
```

Figure 7.23e. Refined associative rules created from the GRI model.

```
File


Results for output field class
    Comparing $A-class with class
        Correct    :      1823     ( 36.46%)
        Wrong      :      3177     ( 63.54%)
        Total      :      5000
        Confidence Values Report for $AC-class
            Range                  : 0.0000 - 0.9800
            Mean Correct           : 0.9494
            Mean Incorrect         : 0.0386
            Always Correct Above   : 0.9800 (18.2% of cases)
            Always Incorrect Below : 0.7400 (61.6% of cases)
            90.0% accuracy above   : 0.0000
            2.0 fold correct above : 0.0000 (68.3% accuracy)
```

Figure 7.23f. Analysis results of using the GRI ruleset.

Mini-Case: Fingerhut Corp.: Leveraging IT Resources in the Mail-order Business

This mini-case here illustrates the design requirements for an application dealing with a vast amount of data that needs to be analysed to extract useful information. The use of a data warehouse to maintain the data allows search of patterns among the data that can be leveraged for more effective marketing practices.

[Source: Pearson, D., *Marketing for Survival*, see http://www.cio.com/archive/]

Fingerhut Corp. is a US $2 billion mail-order business based in Minnesota and employing almost 10,000 people. Fingerhut has relied on an IT-driven strategy to drive their direct marketing efforts. It has mainly accomplished this through the implementation of an enormous data warehouse. The need for a data-warehousing strategy becomes clear when one looks at the product range on offer: it deals with 15,000 products ranging from housewares, electronics, exercise equipment to outerwear and caters to a customer base of around 71 million. A 7-terabyte data warehouse contains data about 2,000 different variables regarding customers. It is this warehouse that is systematically examined for information that could make the company more successful in targetting the specific needs of its diverse customers.

According to David Pearson (1998), Andy Johnson, Senior Vice-president of Market Development, places considerable importance on the data-warehousing capabilities of the organisation. He states that, "[the] group, split between roughly 200 market analysts, 300 creatives (who write, design and produce the catalogues) and 40 statistical scientists, looks to the database for the insights that help the company differentiate itself from competitors. Fingerhut Marketing uses several hundred intricate, proprietary mathematical formulas to segment markets into niches and to make decisions on everything, such as product pricing and creative copywriting in product descriptions."

The data warehouse allows marketers to quickly identify significant new niches in demographics and nuances in customer behaviour making it possible for the company to reach the right customers with the right offering at the right time. It classifies its own customers and customers of other mail-order businesses into groups that are targetted specifically for the customised delivery of product information. The data-warehousing environment is effectively combined with data mining techniques to add value to the organisation's IT efforts.

As an example, Pearson notes, "Fingerhut Marketing recently found that customers who change their residence triple their purchasing in the 12 weeks after their move, with a peak in buying the first 4 weeks. Their selections follow a pattern – they go for furniture, telecommunications equipment and decorations but stay away from jewellery and home electronics. Not a revolutionary finding, but a key one to Fingerhut. The company used the discovery not only to tailor a new 'mover's catalogue' to entice customers who moved but to save money by not sending certain other catalogues during that 12-week window.'

The technology that is used to drive the business is a blend of databases, analysis software and sophisticated graphical user interfaces. According to Pearson, "Fingerhut marketers primarily use point-and-click GUI software from both Software AG Americas Inc. and SAS Institute Inc. Plans call for the company to move its data warehouse from an Oracle relational database-management system in a Sun environment to an IBM Corp. SP multiprocessor super-computer running IBM's DB2. Basic queries, such as the names of all customers who purchased a particular product from a particular catalogue, are available as frequently asked questions (FAQs). To perform more detailed segmentations or test new hypotheses, users formulate ad-hoc mining queries that may combine many disparate variables."

References

Berry, M. J. A. and Linoff, G. (1997) *Data Mining Techniques: For Marketing, Sales, and Customer Support*, John Wiley & Sons Inc., New York

Berson, A. and Smith, S. J. (1997) *Data Warehousing, Data Mining, and OLAP*, McGraw-Hill, New York.

Clementine, see http://www.isl.co.uk/

Dhar, V. and Stein, R. (1997) *Intelligent Decision Support Methods: The Science of Knowledge Work*, Prentice Hall, New Jersey.

Fayyad, U., Piatetsky-Shapiro, G. and Smyth, P. (1996) The KDD process for extracting useful knowledge from volumes of data, *Communications of the ACM*, **39**(11).

Inmon, W. (1992) *Building the Data Warehouse*, QED Technical Publishing Group, Boston, Massachusetts.

Kimball, R. (1996) *The Data Warehouse Toolkit: Practical Techniques for Building Dimensional Data Warehouses*, John Wiley & Sons Inc., New York.

Kingan, R. (1998) Using data mining techniques to support decision making, Unpublished dissertation, University of Auckland.

Microsoft SQL Server 7, see http://www.microsoft.com/

Thomsen, E. (1997) *OLAP Solutions: Building Multidimensional Information Systems*, John Wiley & Sons Inc., New York.

Westphal, C. and Blaxton, T. (1998) *Data Mining Solutions: Methods and Tools for Solving Real-World Problems*, John Wiley & Sons Inc., New York.

Wynkoop, S. (1999) *Using Microsoft SQL Server 7.0*, Que, Indianapolis, Indiana.

DISCUSSION QUESTIONS

1. Identify the data sources that are required to support a key decision process of your choice.
2. What are the different steps that you will undertake to convert these data sources into a form that can be loaded into a data warehouse?
3. Identify facts, dimensions, attributes, etc. for a data-warehouse application that supports the decision process identified above.
4. What would you use to build the application in #3 – ROLAP, MOLAP or HOLAP? Explain your choice.
5. What possible data-mining tasks could be undertaken on the above data warehouse?
6. What data-mining tools could be used to support the tasks identified above?

8
Conclusions and a Look to the Future

8.1 The Ground that We Have Covered

The focus of this book has been on designing systems. This means that we need to explore alternative ways of implementing application systems. There are several ways in which this can be done. For example, a prescriptive approach would be to clearly specify a 'correct' (normative) design approach that could be followed to yield a good design product. In an ideal situation, this would be desirable. Our thinking on design has taken a slightly different approach. We are of the view that when we deal with a class of applications that supports organisational problem solving, we need to be flexible with regard to the design approach. This is in sharp contrast to the normative approach to design. What we are saying is that we need to specify the process in a very abstract and non-prescriptive manner and then follow it up with specific implementation using available technologies. The latter could be delivered in a variety of alternative ways. This would depend on the organisation, the available technologies and the design culture that individuals are used to.

The spirit of the discussion in the preceding chapters captures our approach to designing applications in the context of decision support. At an abstract level, design products should pay particular attention to delivering the capabilities about three main aspects. First, the ability to incorporate data is critical to the successful deployment of these systems. This not only entails the management of storing large volumes of data, but also includes aspects of efficient and innovative means by which the data can be accessed. Second, rules by which data can be manipulated can vary greatly in complexity depending on the task that is being supported. Regardless of whether such rules are simple or complex, a systematic approach to incorporating it in the design product is essential. In our examples, we have focused on the representation and execution dimensions of this problem. A generalisable manipulation ruleset can be represented without paying particular attention to the actual method by which the manipulation will be executed. Hence, we can talk about manipulating data to produce an optimised result by providing a schema for describing the essential manipulation components. This is what we might call a (representation) model Alternatively, we can talk about the specific execution of the manipulation rules – the solving algorithm. In simple cases, the two dimensions might be merged with no loss of meaning. In complex cases, there are many design benefits to be gained by separating the two. The third aspect deals with the ability of the user to appropriately interact with the application. This pertains to user input and application output. More importantly, it refers to the users' ability to specify the essence of a problem (its description) in a manner that is intuitive and yet complete in its specification.

The three aspects referred to above should be juxtaposed against the notion that we need a conceptual-level understanding of our task that should have strong links to implementation technologies (see Figure 3.1). Unless we consciously think about this link, our ability to rapidly translate task requirements to design products is greatly hampered. The way that we have approached this issue is to identify a manageable set of technological platforms that can be linked to the requirements. The specific software tools that were used in the various examples are simply instances of the implementation capabilities that we utilised. This is neither an exhaustive set of software tools nor a most preferred collection. It merely represents a convenient set that can be used to adequately demonstrate the design imperatives under consideration. By restricting the set of software platforms to a few well known and easily available tools, we hope that readers will be encouraged to attempt the design of systems on their own.

8.2 The Rapidly Changing Landscape: The Importance of the Web

Needless to say, information technology is rapidly changing. The lifespans of software tools are highly variable. Even among those tools that endure, successive versions with modified functionality emerge with a high degree of frequency. Hence, it would be wrong to focus exclusively on the specific software platforms that have been used to deliver the examples in this book. These tools are meant to be exemplars that provide the link between capability requirements and deliverables. The requirements are relatively stable over time. The fundamental nature of the problems that are addressed in this book will endure. Addressing these problems through appropriate design will require the identification of the right set of software technologies to match up with the requirements. The task-based focus in this book is meant to convey this point.

Over the past few years, the explosive growth in Internet use has had far-reaching implications for the expectations that organisational users hold regarding computing. Much of the material that we have discussed in this book can be placed in the context of Internet use. The web browser is now a ubiquitous user interface and many of these technologies can be delivered to users through such an interface. The delivery of decision support capabilities via a web browser greatly expands the scope for building and using these applications. A typical organisational application will involve multiple users who are potentially in dispersed locations. An architecture that can deliver the application in such an environment must allow for the possibility that the application and the data exist in a networked environment where users from distributed sites are able to draw on these resources and produce useful results using the familiar web interface.

Such an approach can be implemented by a traditional three-level architecture that is typical of networked environments today. Recall that data is a key component of the applications that we have discussed in this book. It is important to realise that data provided to decision support applications can also serve other applications in a typical organisation. Hence, it is useful to think about implementing the data-oriented issues using a data server. This implementation then allows the data server to act as a provider of data to any application in a network. A similar approach can be used for the applications themselves. Locating applications in application servers in a network makes it accessible to a dispersed community of users who are connected to the network. The users themselves access the applications from network clients using a familiar interface, such as a web browser. This allows for the clients to access powerful capabilities using hardware that is architecturally very simple – the so-called 'thin client'. Many of the applications that we have discussed in this book can be delivered to users within the context of this three-tiered network architecture. Applications and data that support them can reside on powerful application and data servers respectively. Together, they provide services to a set of distributed clients thereby providing a great deal of flexibility in the utilisation of organisation-wide decision support applications.

Examples of integrating large searchable databases using web technology is rapidly becoming familiar to users. Even the most casual of user is adept at using most search engines, using simple word patterns to retrieve an associated set of potentially relevant web pages. This is nothing but a web-based version of electronic library catalogues that users have been familiar with for many years. The success of this strategy to allow users to express retrieval requests within a web-driven environment has been adopted successfully by many well-known electronic commerce applications. For example, the popular book-vendor site Amazon uses precisely such an approach to allow users to construct a request using a form that the users fill in. The parameter values provided by the user are then used to drive a database search to retrieve links to relevant information.

The popularity of the web as a user interface, coupled with available (and rapidly expanding) technologies to deliver data-intensive applications through the web, makes it possible for us to consider this as a viable medium with which to increase the productivity of organisations. The relevant design principle that we should rely on in order to do this is that of integration of discrete components of an application. It should be possible to develop particular aspects of an application in environments that best support those aspects. This is the approach that we have advocated throughout the book. A brief example will help clarify this point. In Chapter 6 we discussed a visual-modelling environment called Visionary that provides access to data-intensive applications that reside in an object-relational database environment. It is possible to integrate a Visionary scene (a problem instance) with a web-based application. This allows users to invoke a web browser from within a Visionary application. It also allows a user to examine a database by invoking a Visionary scene from a web browser. Such capabilities open up a vast array of design possibilities using the ideas that we have discussed throughout this book. It calls for an approach that allows the integration of discretely developed design products into a single powerful application that supports decision making adequately.

8.3 Driving Design from Problems and Tasks

Before we conclude this book, it is important to reiterate what is possibly the single most important design principle that we advocate. The design of decision support applications must rest on an emphasis on decision problems and the associated tasks. The starting point of applications must be the identification and appropriate definition of decision problems. In this book, we have shown a variety of ways by which particular tasks can be addressed using a variety of software technologies. Perhaps, the key influence on successful design lies in the ability of users to structure a decision problem as a collection of implementable tasks. Chapter 4 showed how this can be done by first identifying a problem and then isolating the tasks that make it up. The specific tasks were then taken up as targets for implementation. Too often, application designers are accused of using a particular set of software tools to dictate what the design product will deliver, thereby losing sight of the underlying decision problem that needs to be supported. Figure 3.1 should be used as a guide to drive the design in a top-down approach, where the starting point is the problem itself. The tools are important in the sense that they are the implementation vehicles. However, their role should not extend beyond that. By viewing implementation specifically as the required capabilities to support a well-defined problem, we make it possible to keep the problem itself in sharp focus throughout the design process. Decision-support applications have the real potential to make a dramatic impact on organisation productivity. A disciplined approach to designing such applications is essential to deliver this promise.

Index